CHRISTMAS

DO YOU HEAR ☆ WHAT I HEAR?

BOOKS AUTHORED OR CO-AUTHORED
BY PAUL H. DUNN

You Too Can Teach

The Ten Most Wanted Men

Meaningful Living

Win If You Will

I Challenge You, I Promise You, Vol. 1

Discovering the Quality of Success

Relationships

Anxiously Engaged

The Osmonds

The Birth That We Call Death

Goals

You and Your World

Look at Your World

Life Planning

Dimensions of Life

I Challenge You, I Promise You, Vol. 2

Horizons

Your Eternal Choice

Success Is . . .

The Human Touch

Seek the Happy Life

*Variable Clouds, Occasional Rain,
with a Promise of Sunshine*

Mothers Need No Monuments

The Light of Liberty

PAUL H. DUNN

BOOKCRAFT
Salt Lake City, Utah

Library of Congress Catalog Card Number: 87-71824
ISBN 0-88494-635-5

6th Printing, 1989

Printed in the United States of America

About the Cover

Charles Dickens said: "It is good to be children sometimes, and never better than at Christmastime."

In this family group, Elder Paul H. Dunn is sharing the
true Christmas message with his grandchildren. Kneeling in
front of Elder Dunn is Brandon McIntosh and clockwise in a
circle: Jonathan McIntosh, Tyler Gough, Travis Gough,
Mark Winget, and Adam McIntosh.

Back row, left to right: Carolyn Gough, Brad Winget,
Tamie Winget, and Jeremy Winget.

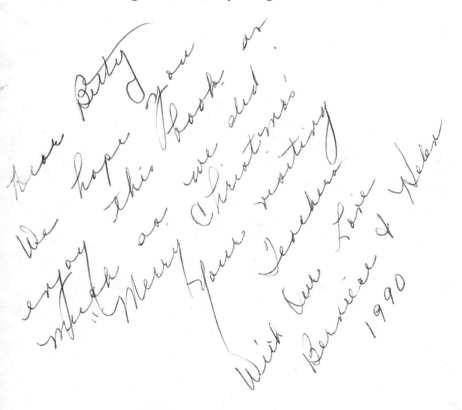

CONTENTS

☆

PREFACE
☆

R. W. Cox observed: "The miracle of Christmas weaves the magic of brotherhood, . . . fills hearts with peace, . . . and causes a weary world to pause . . . to remember . . . and to hope."

We think of Christmas as the day of days. We think of it as the day of the mortal birth of the Holy Child. Yet as important as this event was, it was (and still is) the message of "good tidings," the teachings of the Master, and His triumph over the grave which gave (and still gives) real "joy to the world" when the angel announced, "For unto you is born this day . . . a Saviour, which is Christ the Lord."

While Christ is central to Christmas, many traditions such as Santa Claus, the tree, and the many decorations assist in making the holiday festive and special.

This little volume contains some of the author's feelings and philosophy about Christmas and is not an official publication of the Church.

Once more I express deep appreciation to my secretaries, Elaine Seaman and Sharene Hansen, for wonderful service in their numerous clerical responsibilities. A special thanks to David Christensen for his excellent helps.

Bookcraft and its wonderful staff have once again assisted in so many ways in bringing this project to completion.

For many years and through numerous publications I have enjoyed the insights and expertise of my wife, Jeanne, whose knowledge of words and expression has been most helpful. To her I express my gratitude once more.

PART 1
☆

Hearing the
Babe of Bethlehem

1

KEEPING CHRISTMAS
☆

How are you keeping Christmas this year? The same old way you have every year? You make a list of everybody you need to remember and then start frantically buying gifts, watching for sales, fighting crowds, watching your checkbook empty, seeing your credit cards go over their limit, worrying your way through December, thinking you'll never get finished, and finishing just in time to overeat at the too many parties you're forced to attend. It sounds miserable, and for too many people Christmas has become just that—a time when the spirit of Christmas is just beyond reach, a faint memory through a fog of pressure.

Isn't it ironic that the birth of Christ, which marked the beginning of mankind's ultimate triumph, should be celebrated by a triumph of *things*? It's a time of year when despite our good intentions we exalt tasks above people. There's the mother who, in her scurry to decorate more elaborately than *Home Beautiful* and cook well enough for a Pillsbury bakeoff, yells at her children and sends them away from her in a huff. Didn't she know that all her children really wanted was a happy mother? There's the father who, in desperation because of the financial pinch Christmas imposes, becomes sullen, withdrawn, and terribly worried. And, of course, there's the crowd at the nearest department store, frenetic in their chase for acquisition. They'd fight their neighbor for the last parking place, look desperately for the best bargain, and lose themselves and their best intentions— all just trying to keep Christmas. But in all their efforts, they've actually lost that special spirit. Do you ever feel that way, too?

Can you even remember what everybody gave you last year or the year before that or in 1967? Things don't matter nearly as much as we think they do when we're caught up in the race to get them. Tasks don't matter nearly as much as we think they do when we're caught up in the need to finish them. It's people that matter. It's the warm, whole, happy feeling in our hearts at this time of year that matters. Sometimes it takes less, not more, to make it a full and happy Christmas. It's the little gesture, after all, that clings with us for years after large events have been swept away in our memories.

Evalyn Bennett wrote of a series of small events that happened one Christmas as people at a post office made others more important than their own tasks at hand. She said, "I caught the real spirit of Christmas at the post office [this year]. In that hectic, overcrowded lobby, a concern for total strangers by total strangers was displayed a dozen times during my hour's wait. Christmas chemistry was working like magic and everyone felt it. An elderly woman, obviously not well, was leaning against the wall waiting for someone who was mailing a package. A man at the end of the line stepped out [and] improvised a comfortable seat from a sturdy stand and a telephone book. The woman sank to her perch nodding gratefully.

"A two-year-old was crying as he was being held by his distraught mother. One grandmotherly woman found a box of crackers in a shopping bag; another woman found a key ring to the delight of the child. A man staggered under the load of about fifteen packages. He piled them on the floor with the help of those standing near him. It was a community effort to move the piles along the floor as the line moved forward. There were more hands than were needed to lift the boxes to the counter when his turn came. An Oriental teenager came in, and before long he was telling the woman next to him that this was his first Christmas and how excited he was about it. Everyone within earshot wanted to know more and shouted questions and greetings to him. A woman with arms full of bundles set her young daughter on the desk so the waiting would be easier for both of them. Not a person passed the little girl without a tickle, a question, a comment, or a candy bar. The little girl glowed from all the attention.

"A woman, stooped with age, got to the window and found she needed more staples in her mailing folder. An accommodating employee brought her a stapler, saving her a trip back home. A tough-looking guy in a typical leather jacket stood at the door watching . . . people chattering and laughing. The guy said, 'This is something else. I come from a big city and, believe me, I've never seen anything like this.' " Mrs. Bennett said that, as she concluded her business at the counter, one of the employees smiled and said sincerely, "Have a really good day." She answered, "I already have." (Evalyn Bennett, letter to the editor, *Deseret News*, January 5, 1977.)

It takes so little to make a good day or a merry season. It just takes lifting your eyes from the floor, from self-preoccupation and worry about the hundred trivial things you have to do. Christmas, of all times, is the time to recognize the light in the eyes of the people you pass, a light of recognition that says, "I'm facing what you face. I'm human, too, caught up in the joys and triumphs and struggles of being here."

Can you keep Christmas this year? Henry Van Dyke told us how. He said, "Are you willing to forget what you have done for other people, and to remember what other people have done for you; to ignore what the world owes you, and to think what you owe to the world; to put your rights in the background, and your duties in the middle distance, and your chances to do a little more than your duty in the foreground; to see that your fellowmen are just as real as you are; and try to look behind their faces to their hearts, hungry for joy; to own that probably the only good reason for your existence is not what you are going to get out of life, but what you are going to give to life; to close your book of complaints against the management of the universe, and look around you for a place where you can sow a few seeds of happiness—are you willing to do these things even for a day? Then you can keep Christmas.

"Are you willing to stoop down and consider the needs and the desires of little children; to remember the weakness and loneliness of people who are growing old; to stop asking how much your friends love you, and ask yourself whether you love them enough; to bear in mind the things that other people have to bear on their hearts; to try to understand what those who live in the same house with you really want, without waiting for them to tell you; to trim your lamp so that it will give more light and less smoke, and to carry it in front so that your shadow will fall behind you; to make a grave for your ugly thoughts and a garden for your kindly feelings, with the gate open—are you willing to do these things even for a day? Then you can keep Christmas.

"Are you willing to believe that love is the strongest thing in the world—stronger than hate, stronger than evil, stronger than death—and that the blessed life which began in Bethlehem nineteen hundred years ago is the image and brightness of the Eternal Love? Then you can keep Christmas.

"And if you keep it for a day, why not always?

"But you can never keep it alone." (Henry Van Dyke, as quoted by Richard L. Evans, *Richard Evans' Quote Book* [Salt Lake City: Publishers Press, 1971], p. 240.)

You can never keep Christmas alone. You can never keep it by piling up tinsel-covered things higher and deeper or by smashing through department stores at high speed trying to get all your shopping done in record time. You can only keep Christmas by raising your eyes to look into the faces of the people around you and by seeing the Light of Christ reflected there.

Roy Angell shares this touching account: "A young fellow named Paul received a new automobile from his brother as a Christmas present. On Christmas Eve, when Paul came out of his office, a street urchin was walking around the shiny new car, admiring it. 'Is this your car, mister?' he asked.

"Paul nodded, 'My brother gave it to me for Christmas.'

"The boy looked astounded. 'You mean your brother gave it to you, and it didn't cost you nothing? I wish . . .'

"He hesitated, and Paul knew what he was going to wish. He was going to wish he had a brother like that. But what the lad said jarred Paul all the way down to his heels. 'I wish,' the boy went on, 'that I could be a brother like that.'

"Paul looked at the boy in astonishment. 'Would you like to ride in my automobile?' he asked.

" 'Oh, yes, I'd love that!'

"After a short ride the urchin turned and with his eyes aglow said, 'Mister, would you mind driving in front of my house?'

"Paul smiled a little. He thought he knew what the lad wanted—he wanted to show his neighbors that he could ride home in a big automobile. But Paul was wrong again.

" 'Will you stop right where those two steps are?' the boy asked. He ran up the steps. Then in a little while Paul heard him coming back, but he was not coming fast. He was carrying his crippled brother. He sat him down on the bottom step, then sort of squeezed him, and pointed to the car.

" 'There she is, Buddy, just like I told you upstairs. His brother gave it to him for Christmas, and it didn't cost him a cent, and someday, Buddy, I'm going to give you one just like it! Then you can see for yourself all the pretty things in the Christmas windows that I've been trying to tell you about.'

"Paul got out and lifted the little lad to the front seat of his car. The shining-eyed older brother climbed in beside him, and the three of them began a memorable holiday ride.

"That Christmas Eve Paul learned what Jesus meant when he said, 'It is more blessed to give than to receive.' "

2

"DO YOU HEAR WHAT I HEAR?"

☆

I love Christmas and its music. I especially love to hear the songs of Christmas, even though my own musical talent is somewhat limited.

One of the most popular carols heard during the holidays tells the story of a little shepherd boy:

> Said the little lamb
> To the shepherd boy
> Do you hear what I hear?
> Ringing thru the sky, shepherd boy . . .
> The Child, the Child
> Sleeping in the night
> He will bring us
> Goodness and light.

The song goes on, but even if it didn't those words alone would make me stop to think.

I'm afraid that too often we become so busy at the Christmas season that, if we're not careful, we won't "hear" the message of Christmas. A small shepherd boy heard, and so can we. Allow me to retell the story of a delightful lady who learned, finally, to listen and to hear.

"Next to the Christmas tree was not the girl's bike I'd wanted, but a secondhand boy's bike my father had repainted. Trying to hold back the tears, I thought, 'At least I'll be able to tell the kids at school that I got something "big." ' As a child I never quite got beyond shame and self to the true meaning of Christmas.

"Later, as a teenager, I sang with a group, and Christmas was our busiest time. We sang at company parties, church parties, club parties—and I loved the glamour and the compliments. 'This,' I told myself, 'is the real meaning and feeling of Christmas.' I was wrong again.

"Then one Christmas we decided to sing at the hospital. Each of us bought an inexpensive gift for a patient, and we sang privately to individuals who hadn't had any visitors. While we were singing, one of us would give the gift to that person.

"All the patients seemed responsive except Edgar. He was an old man with tension, fear, and anxiety in his face. He wouldn't look at us at first, but after we sang a couple of songs, he started watching out of the corner of his eye. When I took the little present to him, he broke down and sobbed so hard his whole body shook. Then he said softly, 'You're the only friend I have.' None of us sang the rest of the song, only hummed it in very broken tones.

"Christmas was never the same after that. I forgot all about the present I never received or the places I never went. I still remember and try to recreate the feeling of peace I felt that year." (Karen F. Church, "Who Needs Me at Christmas," *Ensign*, December 1980, p. 48.)

Do you hear what I hear?

I find it interesting that so often we "hear" the message of the Christ child when there is music in the air. Have you ever noticed how often music is used just prior to something really important? I never played a baseball game without hearing the national anthem first. A speaker is often preceded by great music. Many a marriage proposal has been made during the soft strains of a romantic melody. But whatever the case may be, allow me to present my next bit of evidence about "hearing" the message of the babe of Bethlehem. It involves music, and much more. Listen to the words:

"My mother and father, my two little brothers, and I were on a bus during the Christmas of 1944. We had just arrived in the United States and were making our way to Oklahoma.

"The bus was crowded, smoky, and hot. I felt sorry for the extra passengers, mostly servicemen, who had to stand in the aisle. My mother and father struggled with the two children on their laps. Even though night had fallen hours ago, they seemed unable to settle down.

"I looked gloomily out the window at the flatness of the countryside. I longed for home with all the fervor an eight-year-old could muster. At the same time I wondered how I would be accepted at my new school. Worst of all, it did not seem like Christmas, not a bit. The bus lurched slightly, people murmured and stirred, then went back to a stoic endurance. Mother sighed wearily.

"Then a sailor standing in the aisle (and I never did know his name) asked Mother if she thought the baby would come to him. She looked up at him questioningly, made a sudden decision, and gratefully handed the child over. It was obvious that he had held a baby before as he expertly soothed and crooned to him. Around me I saw some of the first smiles of the day as people looked approvingly at the sailor.

"Then he began to sing. Even I recognized 'Silent Night.' Someone joined in, then another and another. As the chorus swelled, contentment rolled like a tangible thing down the aisle and out among the passengers. Everyone felt it. They could not stop with one song.

"I wondered later what had happened. Was it the baby reminding us of that other Babe? Was it the young man—a reaffirmation of the goodness of life in a weary war? Whatever it was, it was the spirit of Christmas to me." (Sherry Downing, "A Sailor Began to Sing," *Ensign*, December 1976, pp. 34–35.)

Do you hear what I hear? Even a child can learn to hear the message of the Savior.

And, speaking of children, when I was much younger there was a song I heard that tells the whole story of "hearing" Christmas. It is short and to the point, and it is absolutely true.

> Why do bells for Christmas ring,
> Why do little children sing?
>
> Once a lovely, shining star,
> Seen by shepherds from afar,
> Gently moved until its light
> Made a manger-cradle bright.
>
> There a darling baby lay
> Pillowed soft upon the hay;
> And the mother sang and smiled,
> "This is Christ, the holy Child."
>
> Therefore bells for Christmas ring,
> Therefore little children sing.
> ("The Holy Child," *The Instructor*, October 1959, p. 334.)

Do you hear what I hear? What is the real message of Christmas?

May I suggest that when we "hear" the Christmas message, we will find it echoed in a thousand different ways. Speaking of children, a close friend shared this true experience.

"I was babysitting with our four older children while my wife took the baby for his check-up. (Babysitting to me means reading the newspaper while the kids mess up the house.) Only that day I wasn't reading, I was fuming. On every page of the paper, as I flicked angrily through them, gifts glittered and reindeer pranced, and I was told there were only six more days in which to rush out and buy what I couldn't afford, and nobody needed. *What,* I asked myself indignantly, *did the glitter and the rush have to do with the birth of Christ?*

"There was a knock on the door of the study where I had barricaded myself. Then Nancy's voice, 'Daddy, we have a play to put on. Do you want to see it?' I didn't! But I had a fatherly responsibility, so I followed her into the living room. Right away I knew it was a Christmas play, for at the foot of the piano stool was a lighted flashlight, wrapped in swaddling clothes, lying in a shoe box.

"Rex, aged six, came in wearing a bathrobe, carrying a mop handle. He sat on the stool, looked at the flashlight. Nancy, aged ten, draped a sheet over her head, stood behind Rex and began, 'I'm Mary, and this boy is Joseph. Usually in this play Joseph stands up and Mary sits down. But Mary sitting down is taller than Joseph standing up, so we thought it looked better this way.'

"Enter Trudy, aged four, at a full run. She has never learned to walk. There were pillowcases over her arms. She spread them wide and said only, 'I'm an angel.'

"Then came Ann, aged eight. I knew right away she represented a Wise Man. In the first place she moved like she was riding a camel (she had on her mother's high-heeled shoes) and she was bedecked with all the jewelry available. On a pillow she carried three items, undoubtedly gold, frankincense, and myrrh. She undulated across the room, bowed to the flashlight, to Mary, to Joseph, to the angel, and to me, and then announced, 'I'm all three Wise Men. I bring precious gifts: gold, circumstance, and mud.'

"That was all. The play was over. I didn't laugh—I prayed. How near the truth Ann was. We come at Christmas burdened down with gold—with the showy gift and the tinsely tree. Under the circumstances of our time and place and custom, we can do no other, and it seems a bit like mud when we think of it.

"But I looked into the shining faces of my children, as their audience of one applauded them, and remembered that a child showed us how these things can be transformed. I remembered that this child came into a material world, and in so doing, eternally blessed that material. He accepted the circumstances, imperfect and frustrating, into which He was born, and thereby infused them with the divine. And as for mud . . . to you and me it may be something to sweep off the rug, but to children everywhere it is something to build with.

"Children see so surely through the tinsel and the habit and the earthly, to the love which in them all strains for expression."

Look around and "hear" the real Christmas. You and I can be a part of it. The "sounds" go something like this:

1. A smile
2. A kind word
3. An unexpected gift
4. A thoughtful act
5. A handclasp
6. A pat on the back
7. A note of thanks
8. A hug
9. An invitation
10. A resolution
11. A surprise visit
12. A person caring

Now, since my family was in the grocery business, let me make that list a "baker's dozen" and add one more:

13. A family get-together

Do you hear what I hear? It's more than "hearing" the music of Christmas. It's more than "hearing" the wrapping of gifts. It's some carolers giving a gift at an old folks' home. It's a sailor holding a baby for an exhausted mom. It's our children and grandchildren reenacting the true story of Christmas. It's you and I as we do numbers one through thirteen on our list. It's the Christ child asking us to make the wonderful sounds of service.

Now, may I conclude with my own assurance that our Savior and Lord was really born. He lives! And He wants us to make proper Christmas sounds so that those around us will hear His message and do His will.

Do you hear what I hear? May we all hear, is my hope for us all!

3

CHRISTMAS . . . AGAIN AND AGAIN!
☆

The Christmas season is wonderful. It seems that for those few short days in December we are on our best behavior. Sales people are more courteous. Policemen are polite. Bosses smile. Dogs bite with less enthusiasm. I have even noticed a greater compatability between teenagers and parents. Imagine!

What is it about the Christmas spirit that causes such changes in behavior? The basic truths of the gospel and our Savior Jesus Christ have undoubtedly become very deep-rooted in our lives as a result of our having been taught of them over the years. Often our feelings about these truths lie dormant. Then that special spirit of Christmas reignites them. Men of great faith in many denominations have had the same feelings. I remember very well the words of Peter Marshall, one of the fine Protestant ministers of our country. His words bear repeating: "Let us not *spend* Christmas and let us not *observe* Christmas, necessarily, but let us *keep* Christmas in our hearts and in our lives."

Jeanne Vinmont shares her experience of keeping "Christmas in our hearts.'' It happened at Christmastime, but it could have been anytime of the year. ''I want to tell you about an incident that happened to me recently as I was doing some Christmas shopping.

"The store was crowded with last-minute shoppers like me. A harried clerk stuffed my purchase into a bag, thrust a wad of bills and change toward me, and rushed away. As I juggled my packages I automatically counted the money in my hand. On the bottom of the stack of bills was an extra ten-dollar bill.

'' 'Keep it,' a voice within me whispered. 'This is a large department store,' I told myself, 'and it can afford the loss. And, besides, everybody does it. It's smart these days to get something for nothing.'

"Even as I reasoned with myself, however, I knew what I would do, for I was suddenly lost in time, remembering an incident that happened almost twenty years before.

"It was December 1943, and I was seven years old. My father was employed by the telephone company in a small farming town in southwest Georgia. My mother was a teacher, and my five-year-old brother and I were happily engrossed in the business of growing up.

"Even though money was scarce and Christmas presents would be small, there was a lot of love and laughter in our family, and my brother and I never felt anything was missing in our life.

"As much as I loved my father, though, I sometimes thought that he expected too much of my brother and me. I had never known my father to be unkind or unfair, but he accepted no excuses for lying, cheating, or dishonesty. I had felt that force of his anger on the seat of my pants on numerous occasions, while I could always find reasons to justify what I considered very minor infractions of the truth. However, I learned the meaning of his lessons on a cold winter night in a way that mere words could never have explained.

"It was raining and dark as we drove to the corner service station. I watched the rain splatter on the hat of old Zeke, the service station attendant, and trickle down his neck as he filled the tank of our car with gas. Zeke shivered in the bitter cold. I was glad when he finished and took the money and ration stamps my father held out the window. In his hurry to get out of the rain, Zeke quickly dropped some change into my father's hand, then disappeared into the service station.

"Our car had already started to roll toward the street when my father suddenly stopped. 'What is it?' my mother asked.

" 'Zeke gave me a nickel too much,' my father answered. 'I'll be right back.'

"With that, he jumped from the car and dashed through the rain into the station.

"Old Zeke was still scratching his head and staring at the nickel in his hand, with a look of utter disbelief on his face, as we drove away.

"My father never mentioned the incident again. In fact, I'm reasonably sure he promptly forgot it. It probably never occurred to him that he was showing my brother and me by example what he expected of us. He was simply doing what he had to do. He could no more have kept that nickel than I could keep the ten dollars I held in my hand.

"With a start, I came back to the present and realized that I was standing before a puzzled clerk who was asking, 'Are you all right, ma'am?'

"As I gave her the ten dollars and explained her mistake, I could almost see my father over my shoulder, smiling and saying, 'That's my girl!'

"Sometimes, even a nickel's worth of honesty goes a long way." (*Better Homes and Gardens*, December 1975, p. 134.)

Such incidents are what make Christmas live every day of the year.

I submit that if a few days of Christmas cheer are good, a month is better. And if one month is good, six are more so. And if six months are good, then why not try for the whole year. Imagine, twelve months of good feelings and Christ-like behavior.

Pearl S. Buck, a great author, has written this tender account of one young man's special Christmas gift that lasted a lifetime, a gift given because of a lesson learned from a loving father.

"He woke suddenly and completely. It was four o'clock, the hour at which his father had always called him to get up and help with the milking. Strange how the habits of his youth clung to him still! His father had been dead for thirty years, and yet he waked at four o'clock in the morning. He had trained himself to turn over and go to sleep, but this morning, because it was Christmas, he did not try. Yet what was the magic of Christmas now? His own children had grown up and gone. He was left alone with his wife. Yesterday she had said, 'Let's not trim the tree until tomorrow, Robert. I'm tired.' He had agreed, and so the tree remained out in the back entry.

"Why did he feel so awake tonight? For it was still night, clear and starry. No moon, of course, but the stars were extraordinary! Now that he thought of it, the stars seemed always large and clear before the dawn of Christmas Day. There was one star now that was certainly larger and brighter than any of the others. He could even imagine it moving, as it had seemed to him to move one night long ago.

"He was fifteen years old and still on his father's farm. He loved his father. He had not known it until one day a few days before Christmas, when he had overheard what his father was saying to his mother.

" 'Mary, I hate to call Rob in the mornings. He's growing so fast and he needs his sleep. If you could see how he sleeps when I go in to wake him up! I wish I could manage alone.'

" 'Well, you can't, Adam.' His mother's voice was brisk. 'Besides, he isn't a child anymore. It's time he took his turn.'

" 'Yes,' his father said slowly. 'But I sure do hate to wake him.'

"When he heard these words, something in him woke: his father loved him! He had never thought of it before, taking for granted the tie of their blood. Neither his father nor his mother talked about loving their children—they had no time for such things. There was always so much to do on the farm.

"Now that he knew his father loved him, there would be no more loitering in the mornings and having to be called again. He got up after that, stumbling blind with sleep, and pulled on his clothes, his eyes tight shut, but he got up.

"And then on the night before Christmas, that year when he was fifteen, he lay for a few minutes thinking about the next day. They were poor, and most of the excitement was in the turkey they had raised themselves and mince pies his mother made. His sisters sewed presents, and his mother and father always bought something he needed, not only a warm jacket maybe but something more, such as a book. And he saved and bought them each something, too.

"He wished, that Christmas he was fifteen, he had a better present for his father. As usual he had gone to the ten-cent store and bought a tie. It had seemed nice enough until he lay thinking the night before Christmas. He looked out of his attic window, the stars were bright. . . .

" 'Dad,' he had once asked when he was a little boy, 'what is a stable?'

" 'It's just a barn,' his father had replied, 'like ours.'

"Then Jesus had been born in a barn, and to a barn the shepherds and the Wise Men had come, bringing their Christmas gifts!

"The thought struck him like a silver dagger. Why should he not give his father a special gift too, out there in the barn? He could get up early, earlier than four o'clock, and he could creep into the barn and get all the milking done. He'd do it alone, milk and clean up, and then when his father went in to start the milking he'd see it all done. And he would know who had done it.

"He laughed to himself as he gazed at the stars. It was what he would do, and he mustn't sleep too sound.

"He must have waked twenty times, scratching a match each time to look at his old watch—midnight, and half past one, and then two o'clock.

"At a quarter to three he got up and put on his clothes. He crept downstairs, careful of the creaky boards, and let himself out. . . . The cows looked at him, sleepy and surprised. It was early for them, too.

"He had never milked all alone before, but it seemed almost easy. He kept thinking about his father's surprise. His father would come in and get him, saying that he would get things started while Rob was getting dressed. He'd go to the barn, open the door, and then he'd go to get two big empty milk cans. But they wouldn't be waiting or empty: they'd be standing in the milk-house filled. . . .

"He smiled and milked steadily, two strong streams rushing into the pail, frothing and fragrant. The task went more easily than he had ever known it to go before. Milking for once was not a chore. It was something else, a gift to his father who loved him. He finished, the two milk cans were full, and he covered them and closed the milk-house door carefully, making sure of the latch. . . .

"Back in his room he had only a minute to pull off his clothes in the darkness and jump into bed, for he heard his father up. He put the covers over his head to silence his quick breathing. The door opened.

" 'Rob!' his father called. 'We have to get up, son, even if it is Christmas.'

" 'Aw-right,' he said sleepily.

"The door closed and he lay still, laughing to himself. In just a few minutes his father would know. His dancing heart was ready to jump from his body.

"The minutes were endless—ten, fifteen, he did not know how many and he heard his father's footsteps again. The door opened and he lay still.

" 'Rob!'

" 'Yes, Dad—'

"His father was laughing, a queer sobbing sort of laugh. 'Thought you'd fool me, did you?' his father was standing beside his bed, feeling for him, pulling away the cover.

" 'It's for Christmas, Dad!'

"He found his father and clutched him in a great hug. He felt his father's arms go around him. It was dark and they could not see each other's faces.

" 'Son, I thank you. Nobody ever did a nicer thing—'

" 'Oh, Dad, I want you to know—I do want to be good!' The words broke from him of their own will. He did not know what to say. His heart was bursting with love.

"He got up and pulled on his clothes again and they went down to the Christmas tree. . . . Oh, what a Christmas, and how his heart had nearly burst again with shyness and pride as his father told his mother and made the younger children listen about how he, Rob, had got up all by himself.

" 'The best Christmas gift I ever had, and I'll remember it, son, every year on Christmas morning, so long as I live.'

"They had both remembered it, and now that his father was dead, he remembered it alone: that blessed Christmas dawn when alone with the cows in the barn, he had made his first gift of true love.

"This Christmas he wanted to write a card to his wife and tell her how much he loved her; it had been a long time since he had really told her, although he loved her in a very special way, much more than he ever had when they were young. He had been fortunate that she had loved him. Ah, that was the true joy of life, the ability to love. Love was still alive in him, it still was.

"It occurred to him suddenly that it was alive because long ago it had been born in him when he knew his father loved him. That was it: love alone could awaken love. And he could give the gift again and again. This morning, this blessed Christmas morning, he would give it to his beloved wife. He could write it down in a letter for her to read and keep forever. He went to his desk and began his love letter to his wife: *My dearest love* . . ." ("Christmas Day in the Morning," as reprinted in *Reader's Digest*, December 1985, pp. 73–76.)

Think of it: "Love alone could awaken love. And he could give the gift again and again."

Why not?

Athletics has taught me that once men and women put their minds to something, it can be done. Babe Ruth was once asked what he thought about when he struck out. "I think about hitting home runs," he answered.

Well, here's our chance. Maybe we can't change the whole world, but we can change ourselves. You and I can decide to make Christmas a year-long proposition.

This world needs more than one day of Christmas. It needs a year. And it can begin with us.

The spirit that Pearl S. Buck and Jeanne Vinmont wrote of can carry over into days, weeks, and months. It can be done. We can do it by continually reminding ourselves of our commitment. Nothing breeds success like success. And in those discouraging moments when it seems useless, a kind Heavenly Father can continue to inspire and lift us.

In reality we can have Christmas again and again. May it be so is my desire for all!

4

DECEMBER'S MAD DASH
☆

As the last week in November closes, it's your last chance to take a deep breath before the busiest time of the year—the holiday season. You remember last year. December was almost too hurried to be fun. There were Christmas cards to mail, presents to be bought for children and family members, outside lights and decorations to hang, parties to attend, food to prepare—and by the time it was all over, you were almost sick with exhaustion. We all begin feeling a little like the mother in this simple tale during the holiday season.

> See Mother. See Mother laugh. Mother is happy.
> Mother has many plans for Christmas.
> Mother is organized. Mother smiles all the time.
> Funny, funny Mother.
>
> See Mother. See Mother wrap presents.
> See Mother look for the end of the Scotch tape roll.

See Mother bite her fingernails.

See Mother go. See Mother go to the store twelve times in one hour.

Go Mother go. See Mother go faster.

Run Mother run.

See Mother trim the tree.

See Mother have a party.

See Mother make popcorn.

See Mother wash the walls.

See Mother scrub the rug.

See Mother tear up the organized plans.

See Mother forget the gift for Uncle Harold.

See the faraway look in Mother's eyes.

Mother has become disorganized.

Mother has become disoriented.

Funny, funny Mother.

Well, male or female, we could all use some tips on how to manage our time to survive December's mad dash. As one writer said, ''Our days are like identical suitcases, all the same size, but some can pack into them twice as much as others.''

Edwin C. Bliss, an expert in time management, gives us these ten ideas to make the most of our minutes (see *Getting Things Done: The ABCs of Time Management* [New York: Charles Scribner's Sons, 1976]).

First, he said, plan your days. Don't become so busy that you crowd out your planning time. The half-hour you spend planning what you'll do with your other twenty-three and one-half is frequently the most valuable part of your day. Make a list and put your most important commitments first. Keep your list with you and follow it.

The number two time-saver, says Bliss, is concentration. If you've made an effective plan for your day, don't distract yourself with worry. Don't think about what you have to do next. That kind of thinking just eats away at your powers and jangles your nerves. Give the project or problem at hand your all-out effort.

Number three time-saver—take breaks. Fatigue cuts down your abilities. When the famous ad says, "You deserve a break today," it's right. It's something like the poem, "A Perfect Day":

> Grandmother, on a winter's day,
> Milked the cows and fed them hay,
> Slopped the hogs, saddled the mule,
> And got the children off to school;
> Did a washing, mopped the floors,
> Washed the windows, and did some chores;
> Cooked a dish of home-dried fruit,
> Pressed her husband's Sunday suit;
> Swept the parlor, made the bed,
> Baked a dozen loaves of bread,
> Split some firewood, and lugged in
> Enough to fill the kitchen bin;
> Cleaned the lamps and put in oil,
> Stewed some apples she thought would spoil,
> Churned the butter, baked a cake,
> Then exclaimed, "For heaven's sake,
> The calves have got out of the pen,"
> Went out and chased them in again;
> Gathered the eggs and locked the stable,
> Back to the house and set the table,
> Cooked a supper that was delicious
> And afterward washed up all the dishes;
> Fed the cat and sprinkled the clothes,
> Mended a basketful of hose,
> Then opened the organ and began to play,
> "When you come to the end of a perfect day."

Years ago when I heard that verse, I thought the only reason Grandmother survived was that she took time off to sing at the end of her day. To be efficient, take breaks.

Number four, avoid clutter. Clean off your desk at the end of the day. Clean off your working space. Give yourself the psychological lift each morning of starting with a neat, well-organized environment. A cluttered environment makes for a cluttered mind.

The number five time-saving rule—don't be a perfection-ist. Certainly set for yourself a standard of excellence, but don't try for the unattainable. Don't be discontented with your best efforts.

The number six time-saving idea—don't be afraid to say no. If you are asked to add to your life another commitment that really isn't in the best interest of yourself or your family, say no. It's the only thing to do.

The number seven time-saving idea—don't procrastinate. Do the most difficult or most unpleasant job first and get it finished so it will no longer plague your mind.

The number eight time-saving idea—delegate some of your work to others who may need or want some additional re-sponsibility. If you have children, give them the chance to become involved in the holiday preparations. They'll love doing some of the jobs that to you may just be additional pres-sure.

The number nine time-saving idea—don't be a worka-holic. More is not always better. At this time of year, every-thing pushes us to do too much. Inspired by magazine layouts of the perfect Christmas, we make too much food, we buy too many presents, we attend too many parties.

But the best time-saving idea is the last one; that is, do radical surgery on your time commitments, especially at this time of year. Analyze your plans for celebrating Christmas and cut out those things that don't really promote your happi-ness and harmony. Have you ever thought how ironic it is that we employ such pomp and ornamentation to celebrate the birth of Jesus Christ, He who chose to live a life of such simplicity and humble service? Could there have been a low-lier birth than his—in a grotto of animals?

To remember Him this Christmas, slow down. Take time to read the scriptures that record His life; gaze at the stars and remember how much you owe Him; laugh and love your family around the glow of a fire; serve someone who needs you.

One woman said, "I used to go home with my young family every Christmas to Mother's. I remember her running out to meet us with hugs; I remember her unhurried delight at small things; I don't recall at all whether the house was freshly scrubbed or the food done up with an ornate flair. But I went home because I felt Christmas there in Mother's love."

Decide now, before it's all upon you, to slow down this season and enjoy Christmas.

5

"I'LL BE HOME FOR CHRISTMAS"
☆

Once in an era many have forgotten, we had a Christmas song. It came to us in a war-torn world, "a million miles west of Pearl Harbor," and we sang it with tears in our eyes because we were pretty sure the song did not tell us the way things really were.

"I'll be home for Christmas. You can count on me. Please have snow and mistletoe and presents 'round the tree. Christmas Eve will find me where the love-light gleams. I'll be home for Christmas if only in my dreams." ("I'll Be Home for Christmas," Walter Kent and Kim Gannon, copyright 1943, 1971, in *200 Deluxe Christmas Songbook for Organ and Piano* [Miami Beach, Florida: Hansen House], p. 28.) And because it was wartime, for many who sang that song it was the last Christmas on this earth.

We would all like to be home for Christmas this season, "where the love-light gleams." Stored in our memories are pleasant moments, warm moments that have touched our hearts and stayed with us forever—the piney smell of the

Christmas tree, the broken ornament that had to be placed on the mantel year after year, the sweet aroma of Christmas cookies baking in the oven, the love in the eyes of dear ones. We remember these times as some of the sweetest in life.

But have you noticed lately that sometimes Christmas isn't quite what you thought it would be? No smell is as pungent, no moment as dear as those you seem to remember. Do you ever feel you have lost something along the way? Do you ever yearn for something and not know what it is?

A small child woke up from a dream and told her father, "I dreamed I was lost and I was scared. I went all over the city looking for my home but I couldn't find it anywhere. I looked at homes of different shapes and sizes but none of them was mine. I asked everyone I saw but no one knew where to find my home."

"I'll be home for Christmas." It is a yearning sort of song. Christmastime itself is a yearning sort of season, and, like this child who dreamed she was lost, we search everywhere to find that sweet something that will make our lives complete—and all the tinsel and presents and sweets will never do it.

The sweet something we long for in our lives can only come from one source—our Heavenly Father and His Son, Jesus Christ, whose very birth we celebrate—and if we ever banish ourselves from that source through indifference, disbelief, or just the daily duties that drive us away from the truly important things, we will never find what we really want in life.

Of course, many believe they have wonderful reasons to forget Jesus Christ at Christmas and all times of life. "I am too busy," says one group. "Who has time for things like that!" "I just can't pray," says someone else. "It doesn't work for me." "I am out for myself," says another and wonders why happiness eludes him.

It reminds me of the Christmas story told by one of the innkeepers who couldn't find room for Joseph and Mary. "What could be done? The inn was full of folk—that they were so important—just the two—no servants, just a workman sort of man leading a donkey and his wife thereon, drooping and pale. I saw them not myself, my servants having driven them away; but if I had seen them, how was I to know?

"Were inns to welcome stragglers up and down in all our towns from Bearsheba to Dan till he should come and how were men to know? There was a sign they say, a heavenly light resplendent, but I had no time for stars; and there were songs of angels in the air out on the hills. But how was I to hear amid the thousand clamors of an inn?"

Christmastime presents a thousand clamors in our lives. Every day of life leaves us saying, as did the innkeeper, "No time for stars or angels' songs." But how foolish this innkeeper seemed when he said, "How was I to know?" How foolish each of us will appear if we cut ourselves off from the Lord—and then, missing it all our lives, can only say, "But how was I to know?"

Make this Christmastime not just a time to receive the socks, ties, bathrobes, and perfume all glittery and wrapped under your tree—receive this Christmas the ultimate gift.

"For God so loved the world, that he gave his only begotten Son, that whosoever believeth in him should not perish, but have everlasting life" (John 3:16).

And the wonder of God's gift to man, even His Only Begotten Son, is not just that this Son was "Wonderful, Counsellor, The mighty God, The everlasting Father, The Prince of Peace"—the wonder is that He was born among us as a little child, that His mother carried Him and nursed Him with loving trust, that He was divine yet subjected Himself to work with common man, that He grew line upon line, that He suffered new pain and sorrow, that His feet grew dusty as He walked the roads of Galilee.

Divine, yes, but since He came as a child and worked with us, His life introduces to us every day the purpose of the sameness in our souls and destinies. He understands our feelings, our needs, our ultimate longings as no one else can.

There is an old story of the Wise Men. Two were old and stern and one was young. As they mounted their camels with their sacks of treasure for Christ, the youngest one stopped them and went into a high chamber where he had not been since he was a child. He rummaged about and presently came out and approached the caravan. In his hand he carried something which glittered in the sun.

The two old Wise Men thought he brought some new gift more rare and precious than any which they had been able to find in all their treasure rooms, but suddenly the young Wise Man took out of his hand a dog made of tin painted white and speckled with black spots where the paint was worn away. The toy shone in the sun as if it had been silver.

The young Wise Man turned a key in the side of the little black and white dog and then he stepped aside. The dog leaped high into the air and turned a somersault. It turned another and another and then rolled over on its side and lay there with its paint shining.

A child, the son of a camel driver, laughed and clapped his hands. He smiled with delight. The old Wise Men, however, were stern.

"What folly has seized you," growled the eldest to the young Wise Man. "Is this a gift to bring to the King of kings?"

And the young man answered and said, "For the King of kings there are true gifts of great worth—gold, frankincense, and myrrh. But this," he said, "is for the child of Bethlehem."

Jesus Christ came to us as a little child; and though he wore the mantle of divinity, He knew the frailties and the longings in each of us. And when we have a yearning and know not what it is for, it could be our souls longing for their heartland, longing to be no longer cut off from the Lord.

"I'll be home for Christmas. You can count on me." As we fill up this sweet season with memories of simple trinkets and carols, let us fill up our souls with the unspeakable joy of knowing that God lives and that this is a time we celebrate His greatest gift—His Son—and that they love us and everyone.

PART 2

☆

Hearing the
Magic of Christmas

6

WHAT THE GRINCH CAN'T STEAL
☆

When my daughters were younger, I used to gather them around me at Christmastime to watch the full-length television cartoon *How the Grinch Stole Christmas*. It is a classic!

The story is about the Grinch who dresses up as Santa and moves through the city of Who-ville taking every package, tree, ornament, and stocking. His goal, of course, is to ruin Christmas and cause as much pain as possible. As he leaves the city, he delights at his "success." Let's recall together those wonderful lines:

> Three thousand feet up! Up the side
>   of Mt. Crumpit
> He rode with his load to the tiptop to
>   dump it!
> "Pooh-pooh to the Whos!" he was
>   Grinch-ish-ly humming.

"They're finding out now that no
    Christmas is coming!
"They're just waking up! I know just
    what they'll do!
"Their mouths will hang open a
    minute or two
"Then the Whos down in Who-ville
    will all cry boo-hoo!

"That's a noise," grinned the Grinch,
"That I simply MUST hear!"

So he paused. And the Grinch put his
    hand to his ear.
And he did hear a sound rising over
    the snow.
It started in low. Then it started to
    grow . . .

But the sound wasn't sad!
Why, this sound sounded merry!
It couldn't be so!
But it WAS merry! Very!

He stared down at Who-ville!
The Grinch popped his eyes!
Then he shook!
What he saw was a shocking surprise!

Every Who down in Who-ville, the
    tall and the small,
Was singing! Without any presents at
    all!
He HADN'T stopped Christmas from
    coming!
IT CAME!

Somehow or other, it came just the
    same!

And the Grinch, with his Grinch-feet
    ice-cold in the snow,
Stood puzzling and puzzling: "How
    could it be so?
"It came without ribbons! It came
    without tags!
"It came without packages, boxes or bags!"

And he puzzled three hours, till his
    puzzler was sore.
Then the Grinch thought of something
    he hadn't before!
"Maybe Christmas," he thought,
    "doesn't come from a store.
"Maybe Christmas . . . perhaps . . .
    means a little bit more!"
(Dr. Seuss, *How the Grinch Stole Christmas*,
New York: Random House, 1957.)

Aren't those great last lines:

"Maybe Christmas," he thought,
    "doesn't come from a store.
"Maybe Christmas . . . perhaps . . .
    means a little bit more!"

And so it does! I submit that Christmas is a spirit, not a
store. It is a feeling, not a present. It is a glow, not a package.

May I suggest that the real spirit of Christmas occurs
wherever there are children present. Now, I don't necessarily
mean children only of a chronological age. I mean children of
whatever age. I am a child, in more ways than one. I love the
smell of a freshly cut Christmas tree as much now as I did as a
boy. It makes no difference to me whether the smell of ham or

turkey occurs now or then. And, as a matter of fact, if there were no ham or turkey it would be all right. There is a spirit about Christmas which almost defies description.

There is a young mother in New Zealand who has captured the essence of Christmas in an experience she has been willing to share:

"We had planned for a long time to help an orphan boy that Christmas, but just could not scrape together enough money. Finally I asked the children how it would be if, instead of Christmas presents, we used the money for that purpose. With a little natural reluctance to waive their traditional rights, the children agreed. But could they have one small gift each in their stockings? It was agreed.

"It happened that we could not obtain a Christmas tree. We parents were willing to let this symbol of Christmas go by the board, but not so the children. The day before Christmas, when I placed on the hearth, beside a jug of flowers and ferns, a gift-wrapped box from a cousin, four-year-old Cerian asked of the fern, 'Is that the Christmas tree?'

" 'No,' I replied, and added on the inspiration of the moment, 'but it will be.' I removed the flowers, replacing them with three tall graceful fronds of asparagus fern cut from the garden, for our Christmas comes in summer. The children were delighted and decorated the delicate bush lightly with tinsel strands.

"Then the small miracle began. The children began searching in drawers and closets for gifts to give each other, and placed them under the tree. When these sources failed to yield further treasure, meager pocket money was taken to the store and, for the first time, spent on others.

"When seven people give to seven people, things multiply. Done up gaily in last year's reused wrapping paper, the gifts for our giftless Christmas spread from under the tree across the floor. The spirit of Christmas, which in more affluent years we had tried in vain to cultivate, now, as the power of money went out the window, came stealing softly in the door." (Rosemary Petty, "Asparagus Fern Christmas," *Ensign*, December 1976, p. 36.)

Isn't it amazing what can happen in our lives when the real spirit of Christmas moves in? Money, position, status mean nothing when that holy feeling enters our hearts. Having spent three Christmases amid the battles of a world war, I can testify that even under conditions as adverse as those there is a spirit of Christmas as real as you and I.

I'm not sure who wrote it, but I recently came upon a description of the Christmas spirit which is better than anything I have ever found. Whoever wrote it may be "anonymous" to us, but he or she certainly was not anonymous to the Lord. It was written with His Spirit:

"I'm the Christmas Spirit. I enter the home of poverty and cause pale-faced children to open wide their eyes in pleased wonder. I cause the miser to release his clutched hand, thus painting a bright spot upon his soul.

"I cause the aged to remember their youth and to laugh in the glad old way. I bring romance to childhood and brighten dreams woven with magic.

"I cause eager feet to climb dark stairways with filled baskets, leaving behind hearts amazed at the goodness of the world.

"I cause the prodigal to pause in his wild and wasteful way and send to anxious loved ones some little token which releases glad tears, washing away the hard lines of sorrow.

"I enter dark prison cells, causing scarred manhood to remember what might have been and pointing to better days yet to come.

"I enter the still white home of pain, and there lips that are too weak to speak just tremble in silent, eloquent gratitude.

"In a thousand ways I cause this weary old world to look up into the face of God and for a few moments forget everything that is small and wretched. You see I am the Christmas Spirit." (Author unknown.)

But before going any further, may I emphasize that the spirit of Christmas is, in fact, the Spirit of Christ. It is because of Jesus that these feelings are real. Even children recognize the true spirit and meaning. Jack Smith shares this account of love and Christmas feelings.

"I didn't question Timmy, age nine, or his seven-year-old brother, Billy, about the brown wrapping paper they passed back and forth between them as we visited each store.

"Every year at Christmastime, our service club takes the children from poor families in our town on a personally conducted shopping tour. I was assigned Timmy and Billy, whose father was out of work. After giving them the allotted four dollars each, we began our trip. At different stores I made suggestions, but always their answer was a solemn shake of the head, no. Finally I asked, 'Where would you suggest we look?'

" 'Could we go to a shoe store, sir?' answered Timmy. 'We'd like a pair of shoes for our daddy so he can go to work.'

"In the shoe store the clerk asked what the boys wanted. Out came the brown paper. 'We want a pair of work shoes to fit this foot,' they said.

"Billy explained that it was a pattern of their daddy's foot. They had drawn it while he was asleep in a chair.

"The clerk held the paper against the measuring stick, then walked away. Soon, he came with an open box. 'Will these do?' he asked.

"Timmy and Billy handled the shoes with great eagerness. 'How much do they cost?' asked Billy.

"Then Timmy saw the price on the box. 'They're $16.95,' he said in dismay. 'We only have $8.00.'

"I looked at the clerk, and he cleared his throat. 'That's the regular price,' he said, 'but they're on sale: $3.98, today only.'

"Then, with shoes happily in hand the boys bought gifts for their mother and two little sisters. Not once did they think of themselves.

"The day after Christmas the boys' father stopped me on the street. The new shoes were on his feet, gratitude was in his eyes. 'I just thank Jesus for people who care,' he said.

" 'And I thank Jesus for your two sons,' I replied. 'They taught me more about Christmas in one evening than I had learned in a lifetime.' "

Such is the spirit of Christmas. Moms and dads feel it. Kids feel it. Brothers and sisters feel it. The rich feel it, as do the poor; the single as well as the married; the illiterate as well as the educated.

What the Grinch couldn't steal, no man can. It is ours for the asking. The only demand made on us by the Lord is that when we receive it, we must share. So let's share! With our family; with our friends; with those we don't know; with those we do know.

May each of us allow that spirit to enter our hearts and our homes and ponder the words of that great Christmas carol, "O Little Town of Bethlehem":

> How silently, how silently
> The wondrous gift is given!
> So God imparts to human hearts
> The blessings of his heaven.
> No ear may hear his coming;
> But in this world of sin,
> Where meek souls will receive him, still
> The dear Christ enters in.

May we truly allow him to enter.

7

IN DEFENSE OF SANTA
☆

At our house, like yours, we share lots of Christmas traditions. One is that my wife loves to decorate the house and create wonderful feelings. Another is to share stories both real and mythical in creating a spirit of good will and anticipation. While the emphasis is on our Lord and Savior, we have always felt there was a place for Santa.

Let me share several of our favorite stories:

"Mrs. Santa was so tired. She sat down in her little rocking chair and started to rock to and fro before the fire. She had worked hard to get Santa and his reindeer on their way, and now that they were gone, she could sit and rest.

"She had just dropped off to sleep when the telephone rang. She awoke with a start, blinked her eyes, and wondered what had awakened her. The telephone rang again, and she quickly lifted the receiver and said, 'Hello.'

"A very little voice answered and said, 'Is Santa Claus there?'

" 'No,' she replied, 'he has gone, but this is Mrs. Santa.'

" 'This is Elizabeth,' said the very little voice. 'I wanted to tell Santa Claus about Jane. Jane doesn't even believe there is a Santa Claus. I thought maybe if Santa knew about her, he would leave her something so she would know about him.'

"Without even thinking what she was saying, Mrs. Santa replied, 'We will leave her something, never you fear.'

"When she heard the click of the receiver and realized what she had promised Elizabeth, Mrs. Santa was very worried. 'What in the world will I do? Santa is gone; the Brownies are all out, and no one is here but Blitzen, who had to stay home because he sprained his ankle on the North Star.'

"Mrs. Santa finally realized that if anything were to be done, she would have to do it. And she would have to do it on the only night in the year when she could sit with her hands folded and rock to and fro before the fire.

"She picked up a doll's body that she had thrown away because it insisted on saying 'Pa-Pa' instead of 'Ma-Ma' as all dolls should do. She took it out into the workshop where she found a doll's head. With a little paint and a little hair that she found, she made the doll look pretty.

"She made a dress out of a small piece of pink satin and trimmed it with yards and yards of lace. When she was through, Mrs. Santa looked at the doll and said, 'It is pretty enough to delight the heart of any girl, except for the fact, of course, that it says "Pa-Pa" instead of "Ma-Ma" as all dolls should do.'

"Suddenly, she heard the cock crow. This startled her for Mrs. Santa knew that in another hour Jane would be climbing out of bed. She went to the stable and hitched lame Blitzen to the sled Santa had discarded ten years before, and away they went, clippity-cloppity-hop, hoppity-hippity-clip, as fast as poor Blitzen could go.

"Finally, just as the sun was peeking over the hill with a broad shining grin, Mrs. Santa put the doll on a chair by the side of Jane's bed. Then she and Blitzen hurried back to their home at the North Pole.

"She just had time enough to get Blitzen unhitched and into his stable, and herself into bed before Santa came in.

"He came in very quietly so as not to disturb her and said, 'This is the only night of the year when my poor Mrs. Santa has nothing to do but just sit and rock to and fro in front of the fire.' " (Mary Pratt Parrish, "Mrs. Santa's Night Off," *Children's Friend*, December 1964, pp. 18–19.)

Now, let's share another story I often tell my grandchildren. It's from Luke and has been told over and over and over again.

"And it came to pass in those days, that there went out a decree from Caesar Augustus, that all the world should be taxed.

"(And this taxing was first made when Cyrenius was governor of Syria.)

"And all went to be taxed, every one into his own city.

"And Joseph also went up from Galilee, out of the city of Nazareth, into Judaea, unto the city of David, which is called Bethlehem; (because he was of the house and lineage of David:)

"To be taxed with Mary his espoused wife, being great with child.

"And so it was, that, while they were there, the days were accomplished that she should be delivered.

"And she brought forth her firstborn son, and wrapped him in swaddling clothes, and laid him in a manger; because there was no room for them in the inn.

"And there were in the same country shepherds abiding in the field, keeping watch over their flock by night.

"And, lo, the angel of the Lord came upon them, and the glory of the Lord shone round about them: and they were sore afraid.

"And the angel said unto them, Fear not: for, behold, I bring you good tidings of great joy, which shall be to all people.

"For unto you is born this day in the city of David a Saviour, which is Christ the Lord.

"And this shall be a sign unto you; Ye shall find the babe wrapped in swaddling clothes, lying in a manger.

"And suddenly there was with the angel a multitude of the heavenly host praising God, and saying,

"Glory to God in the highest, and on earth peace, good will toward men.

"And it came to pass, as the angels were gone away from them into heaven, the shepherds said one to another, Let us now go even unto Bethlehem, and see this thing which is come to pass, which the Lord hath made known unto us.

"And they came with haste, and found Mary, and Joseph, and the baby lying in a manger." (Luke 2:1–16.)

Is there a place in the true spirit of Christmas for both Santa and Christ? I personally believe there is.

I have heard some voice concern about Santa Claus and the commercialization that accompanies him. Some would question Santa's appearing in a "religious" book on Christmas.

May I be one voice in defense of Santa. Although some parents may not handle St. Nick very well, and although some children have been disappointed on Christmas morning because of him (or is it because of others?), Santa can wield a powerful influence for good. David O. McKay put it about as well as it can be stated. His words express how I feel:

"It is a glorious thing to have old St. Nicholas in our hearts and in our homes today, whether he enters the latter through the open door or creeps down the chimney on Christmas Eve. To bring happiness to others without seeking personal honor or praise by publishing it is a most commendable virtue. . . .

"Good old St. Nicholas has long since gone the way of all mortals, but the joy he experienced in doing kindly deeds is now shared by millions who are learning that true happiness comes only by making others happy—the practical application of the Savior's doctrine of losing one's life to gain it. In short, the Christmas spirit is the Christ spirit, that makes our hearts glow in brotherly love and friendship and prompts us to kind deeds of service." (*Gospel Ideals*, pp. 550–52.)

May I suggest that, handled properly, Santa Claus can be a great help to the Christ child. To hold a child's hand and watch him searching for just the right gift for his mom, or watching children wide-eyed as they come to take their parents to the front room on Christmas morning is something due in part to Santa and the spirit so well described by President McKay.

Another leader and personal friend, President Harold B. Lee, told a story that could never have been enjoyed without the celebration of Christ's birth. The *true* spirit of Santa is also evident everywhere.

"Sobbing, they said: 'Our friends did not have any Christmas. Santa Claus did not come to their home.'

"All too late we remembered that just across the street was a family whose father was not a member of the Church, although the children were, and the mother passively so; he had been out of work, and we had forgotten. Our Christmas was spoiled.

"We sent for those children and tried to divide what we had in an attempt to make up for our lack of thoughtfulness, but it was too late. Christmas dinner that day did not taste very good to me."

As a young stake president, Elder Lee determined not to let that scene be repeated.

"We knew that we had about one thousand children under ten years of age for whom, without someone to help them, there would be no Christmas.

"We started to prepare. We found a second floor over an old store on Pierpont Street. We gathered toys, some of which were broken, and for a month or two before Christmas, fathers and mothers were there. Some arrived early or stayed late to make something special for their own little ones.

"That was the spirit of Christmas giving—one only had to step inside the door of that workshop to see and feel it. Our goal was to see that none of the children would be without Christmas.

"There was to be Christmas dinner in all the homes of the

4,800 who, without help, wouldn't have Christmas dinner. Nuts, candy, oranges, a roast, and all that went with it would be their Christmas menu.

"It so happened that I was then one of the city commissioners. On the day before Christmas that year we had had a heavy snowstorm, and I had been out all night with the crews getting the streets cleared, knowing that I would be blamed if any of my men fell down on the job. I had then gone home to change my clothes to go to the office.

"As I started back to town, I saw a little boy on the roadside, hitchhiking. He stood in the biting cold, with no coat, no gloves, no overshoes. I stopped, and he climbed into the car beside me.

" 'Son,' I asked, 'are you ready for Christmas?'

" 'Oh golly, mister, we aren't going to have any Christmas at our home. Daddy died three months ago and left Mama and me and a little brother and sister.'

"Three children, each under ten!

" 'Where are you going, son?'

" 'I'm going up to a free picture show.'

"I turned up the heat in my car and said, 'Now, give me your name and address.'

"Further conversation revealed that they were not members of the Church.

" 'Somebody will come to your home; you won't be forgotten. Now, you have a good time today—it's Christmas Eve.'

"That night I asked each bishop to go with his delivery men and see that each family was cared for, and to report back to me.

"While waiting for the last bishop to report, I painfully remembered something. In my haste to see that all my duties at work and my responsibilities in the Church were taken care of, I had forgotten the boy in my car and the promise that I had made.

"When the last bishop reported, I asked, 'Bishop, have you enough left to visit one more family?'

" 'Yes, we have,' he replied.

"I told him the story and gave him the address.

"A little later he called to say that that family too had received some well-filled baskets. Christmas Eve was over at last, and I went to bed."

St. Nick is responsible, in large part, for the traditional giving of gifts. It's a wonderful tradition. So, in my defense of Santa, I suggest that we place responsibility for "his short-comings" where it really belongs—not on Santa but on our-selves. You and I *can* use Santa to help develop the true spirit of Christ and Christmas.

I have a friend with whom I was discussing this issue one time. He was somewhat cynical about the overweight fellow in red, but he made a great statement worth repeating. He said, "I have sometimes witnessed a wonderful balance be-tween the worship of Jesus Christ and the spirit of giving exemplified in Santa." Well said, my friend!

I know from practical experience that the day we celebrate as the birthday of Christ can be celebrated reverently, and, at the same time, the spirit of Santa can also be enjoyed. My parents did it for me, and I have seen our children and their children find the same balance. May we all do so. May we use Santa Claus properly in the celebration of Christmas.

8

THE SPIRIT OF GIVING
OR THE SANTA
WITHIN US
☆

Jay Frankston, who is Jewish, once observed: "There's nothing so beautiful as a child's dream of Santa Claus." He remembers how sad he felt as a boy when Christmas was everybody else's holiday and how he felt left out. It wasn't toys he yearned for: it was Santa Claus and a Christmas tree. When he got married and had children, he decided to make up for what he had missed.

He started with a seven-foot tree, all decked out with lights and tinsel, with a Star of David on top to soothe those whose Jewish feelings would be disturbed by the display.

But something was missing he recalls, something big and round and jolly, with jingle bells and a ho! ho! ho! He bought some bright red cloth and his wife made an authentic costume. He played Santa for his children for several years, and each year he noticed the awe and saw in their eyes the fantasy and magic of what he had become. Santa was special. He was the personification of kindness and gentleness.

One winter day he noticed a little girl trying to reach a mailbox slot, and saying, "Mommy, are you sure Santa will get my letter?" His mind began to whirl. He wondered, *Whatever becomes of all those letters children write?* The postal service answered his inquiry, telling him the dead letter office stored thousands of such letters in huge sacks.

With permission from postal authorities, he began rummaging through the letters and was disturbed at the demands and greed of so many spoiled children. Most of the letters were gimme, gimme, gimme requests. But one particular letter caught his attention. It was different. It read: "Dear Santa, I am an eleven-year-old girl and I have two little brothers and a baby sister. My father died last year and my mother is sick. I know there are many who are poorer than we are and I want nothing for myself, but could you send us a blanket 'cause Mommy's cold at night.'' It was signed Suzy.

Frankston was so moved he dug deeper into those sacks and found eight such letters. He took them and went straight to the Western Union office and sent each child a telegram. "Got your letter. Will be at your house. Wait for me. Santa."

While he knew he could not fill all their needs, he could bring them home. He budgeted $150 and bought some presents. On Christmas day his wife drove him around, and his first call took him to the outskirts of the city. The letter from Peter Barski had read:

"Dear Santa, I am ten years old and I am an only child. We've just moved to this house and I have no friends yet. I'm not sad because I'm poor but because I'm lonely. I know you have many people to see and you probably have no time for me. So I don't ask you to come to my house or bring anything. But could you send me a letter so I know you exist?"

"Dear Peter," his telegram began. "Not only do I exist, but I'll be there on Christmas Day. Wait for me." Peter's house was wedged between two tall buildings. Its roof was of corrugated metal and it was more of a shack than a house. With a bag of toys slung over his shoulder, Frankston walked up the steps and knocked. A heavyset man opened the door. His hand went to his face in astonishment. "Please," he stuttered, "The boy is—at mass. I go get him. Please wait." He threw on a coat and, assured that "Santa Claus" would wait, ran down the street.

As Frankston stood in front of the house waiting, he noticed another shack across the street. Through the front window he could see little black faces peering at him and tiny hands waving. The door opened shyly and some voices called out, "Hi ya, Santa."

He said he ho! ho! ho'd his way across the street, and a woman asked him to come in. Inside were five children from one to seven years old. He spoke to them of Santa and the spirit of love, which is the spirit of Christmas. Then, seeing the torn Christmas wrapping, he asked if they liked what Santa had brought them. Each thanked him—for the socks, the sweater, and warm underwear. "Didn't I bring you any toys?" he remarked. They shook their heads sadly. "Ho! Ho! Ho! I slipped up," he said. "We'll have to fix that!" Knowing that he had extra toys in the car, he gave each child a toy. There was joy and laughter, but when Santa got ready to leave, one little girl was crying. "What's the matter," Santa asked. "Oh, Santa!" she sobbed. "I'm so happy!" The tears also rolled from Santa's eyes.

As he stepped outside, "Panie, panie, prosye . . . Sir, sir, please," he heard Mr. Barski say across the way. Peter just stood there and looked as Santa walked into the house. "You came," he said. "I wrote and . . . you came." When Peter recovered, Santa spoke with him about loneliness and friendship, and gave him a chemistry set and a basketball. He thanked Santa profusely. And his mother asked something of her husband in Polish. Frankston's parents were Polish, so he spoke a little and understood a lot.

"From the North Pole," he said in Polish. She looked at him in astonishment. "You speak Polish?" "Of course," he said. "Santa speaks all languages." With that he left them in joy and wonderment.

For many years Jay Frankston listened to the cries of children muffled in unopened envelopes, and answered as many as he could. What a tremendous example of a true giver. (See

Jay Frankston, *A Christmas Story* [New York: Summit Books, 1977].)

The Apostle Paul, writing to the Corinthians, counseled: "So let him give; not grudgingly, or of necessity: for God loveth a cheerful giver" (2 Corinthians 9:7).

Sometimes it may become difficult to give when we feel we ourselves are in need just as much, whether it be food, clothing, money, or our time when we are in a hurry. If there are those moments when we resent giving, recall the admonition of the Lord to such givers: "It is counted unto him the same as if he had retained the gift" (Moroni 7:8).

Giving is one thing. Giving cheerfully is quite another.

Here is another wonderful example of the spirit of giving— rather, an example of "cheerful giving." The young woman who experienced this special Christmas Eve will never be the same.

"Our new neighbor was a Mexican national, working for some Californians who owned a dairy farm in our little town of Weston, Idaho. He had arrived there to begin work early in November. With him had come his beautiful dark-eyed family. None of them could speak English. His lonely wife had lasted in this cold foreign place slightly more than a month, and then she had gathered her little ones and fled back to a warmer climate and to her family.

"The poor husband was left alone. He seemed like a very ambitious man, working from early morning to late at night. But he also seemed very gruff. Any attempts at communication had proved futile, even unwelcome. So here it was Christmas Eve, and there was a neighbor all alone in his quiet house, without a sign of Christmas anywhere.

" 'I don't suppose he even has anything good to eat tonight,' Mom commented. We looked at each other, then the idea began to snowball. Here we were in the midst of plenty. We could share. We *would* share. My sisters, Jill and Meridee, became exuberant. They were giggling and planning when someone (perhaps pessimistic me) almost burst their balloon. Would our offering be wanted or even

accepted? From past experience this possibility seemed unlikely.

"Then Daddy counseled wisely, 'Why wouldn't it be
wanted and appreciated? This neighbor, even though a gruff
stranger, is a brother—another child of God. And tonight he is
a very lonely child of God.'

"So we went on with our planning and preparations. Soon
we had plates heaping with scrumptious holiday food,
covered with napkins to keep it warm. As we girls grabbed
our coats, another question was posed. How could we make
the man understand our mission? Since he didn't speak English, would he know what we were saying when we chorused,
'Merry Christmas'?

"Bravely I countered, 'Don't worry. After all, I have
studied Spanish for two whole quarters at the university. I am
practically an expert!'

"So off we went—a parade of nervous, giggling females
bearing gifts, stumbling and slipping in the snow, but determined to let our lonesome neighbor know that someone was
thinking of him this Christmas Eve.

"Suddenly I found myself shoved to the front of the pack
at his door. I knocked, and after what seemed forever we
heard a shuffling, and then the door opened a suspicious
crack. We shrank back momentarily, but then our courage
soared and we started to say, 'Merry Christmas.' He looked
puzzled, but he opened the door wide. The light from his
lamp illuminated us, and shyly we held out the plates we had
brought. He looked at us. We looked at him. Nobody moved.
What were we to do?

"Then it hit me. 'Feliz Navidad'—the Spanish Christmas
greeting we had learned in class. I choked out something that
sounded like 'Feliz Navidad,' and he began to smile, a big,
beautiful Christmas Eve smile.

" 'Feliz Navidad,' he sort of whispered. Then everyone
started saying 'Feliz Navidad.' We were smiling, we were
laughing, we were almost crying as we shared the spirit of the
occasion.

"Then he looked at the plates and motioned for us to come in. So in we went. After depositing the food on a nearby table, we turned to leave, and he followed us out saying over and over, "Muchas gracias, muchas gracias." Then the door closed.

"We looked at one another and began to laugh, and we hugged each other. It had been so much fun—the best time ever. The very best of many wonderful, happy Christmases." (Tedra Merrill Balls, "Feliz Navidad!" *Ensign*, December 1976, pp. 35–36.)

There's nothing like a cheerful giver!

Every time I pick up a Christmas card I am reminded of this principle of "a cheerful giver." It was the cheerful desire of a young teenager that brought Christmas cards into being (teenagers can and do give willingly). Young William Egley was an apprentice in an English engraving shop in 1842. He loved his employer and family but had nothing to give them at Christmastime that year. So, unable to buy anything, this great young man came up with an ingenious idea. I take just an excerpt from his story:

"Slowly, Will went to his room, his Christmas spirit almost sapped by the unhappy thought that he had nothing to give. He sat in the chilly room, his candle flaring on the table, and looked about him at his worldly possessions—his clothing, a miniature of his dead mother, which his father had done in delicate pastel shades, and the paints his father had given him. Like his father, Will had early shown a talent in art, and he was the proudest fellow for miles around when his father presented him with some art materials.

"For Will the most treasured gift in the world was a picture.

"Gift? Gift! Suddenly the boy stood up straight, fired with an idea. A picture! He would paint a picture for the Broadbents for Christmas.

"Excitement made his cold hands tremble a little as he arranged his materials and began to work.

"The next morning when he heard the merry calls of the family on Christmas Day, Will hurried out of bed and took his picture down, presenting it to Mr. Broadbent apologetically. "It's not much, but here's a Christmas greeting for the family."

"They all admired the picture of a family gathered around a heavily laden dinner table. On one side was a group of carolers and on the other a skating scene, all done in the reds and greens of the holiday season. Under the three panels so typical of the holiday in England, he had written in large letters: 'A Merry Christmas and a Happy New Year.'

" 'That's the most Christmassy present I've ever seen,' said Elizabeth.

" 'Indeed it is,' Mr. Broadbent chuckled. 'What a pity more people don't receive greetings from their friends at Christmastime.'

" 'I guess people wouldn't have time to make very many each year,' Will said.

"Then the boy found Mr. Broadbent looking at him in a strange and serious way. 'Come, come, lad!' he said. 'They can be lithographed.' " (Louise D. Morrison, "The First Christmas Greeting," *Children's Friend*, December 1961, pp. 40–42.)

And so it was. That next year William Egley made up a sketch which was lithographed and then filled in with colors. From the simple desire of a young man to be a "cheerful giver" came one of the really great Christmas traditions we enjoy.

I conclude with a little practical counsel. There is no doubt that Christmas brings out the best in most of us. There is an occasional Scrooge, but most of us want to do the right thing. Allow me to make two suggestions about being a cheerful giver:

First, let's remember that gifts don't always have to be "things." We all see so much depression at Christmastime because people go into debt trying to give "things." It's hard to be a cheerful giver when we're always unhappy with the gift we give, or because we can't give more. Let's give what we can, but when we don't have much to give, we can give ourselves. A homemade offering is a great thing. A note or a letter of love and appreciation can't be purchased with money; a promise to be more patient needs very little gift-wrapping to be beautiful; spending more time with each other requires no financial investment. The list has no end.

Second, to make sure we are "cheerful givers," let's spend a little time remembering the most cheerfully given gift of all. How about rereading the Christmas story in Luke? Or how about a few, quiet moments of meditation and thought about our Elder Brother? How about some constant prayers on the subject? Or how about a family discussion about the Savior?

Being a father and grandfather has given me greater understanding of what it means to be a cheerful giver. Children have a way of giving that makes sense. They simply give because they want to.

May you and I learn to do the same thing. May we give willingly and cheerfully. As we do so, I bear testimony that our gifts will be acceptable to those who receive them, and above all else, to the Greatest Giver of all.

9

GETTING YOUR HEART FIXED

☆

Some years ago, near a seldom-used trail in the Amargosa Desert in California, there stood a rundown hut. Nearby was a well, the only source of water for miles around. Attached to the pump was a tin baking powder can with a message inside written in pencil on a sheet of brown wrapping paper.

This was the message: "This pump is all right as of June, 1932. I put a new sucker washer into it and it ought to last five years. But the washer dries out and the pump has got to be primed. Under the white rock I buried a bottle of water, out of the sun and cork end up. There's enough water in it to prime this pump but not if you drink some first. Pour in about ¼ and let her soak to wet the leather. Then pour in the rest medium fast and pump [like crazy]. You'll git water. The well never has ran dry. Have faith.

"When you git watered up, fill the bottle and put it back like you found it for the next feller.

"Signed: Desert Pete

"P.S. Don't go drinking the water first! Prime the pump with it and you'll git all you can hold. And next time you pray, remember that God is like the pump. He has to be primed. I've given my last dime away a dozen times to prime the pump of my prayers, and I've fed my last beans to a stranger while saying amen. It never failed yet to git me an answer. You got to git your heart fixed to give before you can be give to." (*Bits and Pieces*, January 1983, pp. 19–20.)

What a message in that story! "You got to git your heart fixed to give before you can be give to."

If Paul's words concerning Christ are true and we know that "it is more blessed to give than to receive" (Acts 20:35), then we must learn how to give, and give with the proper spirit.

As I think back to my boyhood days and all those great Christmases, I realize something now that I had yet to learn then—that as much as I thought at the time that I was enjoying and appreciating my many presents, I never actually got the thrill from them that I did from gifts received later in life after I had learned the joy of giving first and *then* receiving.

And while speaking of the importance of giving, another principle needs to be noted here, that of learning to be gracious receivers as well as unselfish givers. I think many of us find ourselves unable to appreciate gifts given and kind deeds shown for fear our motives will be misunderstood. How disappointing, however, for a sincere giver not to sense appreciation and joy from one he has attempted to please or to assist!

So the ability to give and to receive go hand in hand to bring about a great joy and satisfaction, as the following example shows.

"There are two seas in Palestine. One is a body of fresh water with fish in it. Splashes of green adorn its banks. Trees spread their branches over it and stretch out their thirsty roots to sip its cooling waters. Along the shore the children play as children played when the Savior was there. He loved it. He could look across its silver surface when he spoke his parables, and on a rolling plain not far away he taught and fed five thousand people. The river Jordan helps create this sea with sparkling water from the hills. So it flourishes in the sunshine; and men build their homes near it and birds, their nests, and every kind of life is happier because it is there. The river Jordan flows on south into another sea. Here is no splash of fish, no fluttering of leaf, no song of birds, no children's laughter. Travelers choose another route unless on urgent business. The air hangs heavy above its waters, and neither man nor beast nor fowl will drink.

"What makes the difference in these two neighboring seas? Not the river Jordan. It empties the same good water into both. Not the soil in which they live. Not the country round about. The difference is this: the Sea of Galilee receives, but does not keep, the Jordan. For every drop that flows into it, another flows out. The giving and receiving go on in equal measure. The other sea is shrewder, hoarding its income jealously. It will not be tempted into generous impulse. Every drop it gets, it keeps. The Sea of Galilee gives and lives; the other sea gives nothing."

Like the two seas in Palestine, I believe that there are two kinds of people. Those who learn to give as well as receive are generally happy. Those who don't learn that lesson are forever searching and grabbing and do not find fulfillment.

Ebenezer Scrooge was fortunate in Dickens' *A Christmas Carol*. At first he was a dead sea if ever there was one. His whole life was spent in hoarding. But then he had a chance to change, and he had the sense to do so. He let out the dams and the dikes and let his rivers flow. The more he let out, the more that came in. That story is a classic. *A Christmas Carol* is a popular Christmas story not only because it is well written but also because the principles contained therein are true.

As I have pondered the principle of "getting your heart fixed to give before you can be give to," my mind has been turned to those times I have been allowed to see it in action. At Christmastime my heart has often gone back to days in the military. Over the years I have shared personal experiences of the Christmas spirit in time of war. But rather than tell my own story again, I think it would be appropriate to share one told by a fellow soldier. It was in his war that he learned first hand the power of giving. He relates:

"I had never seen the spirit of Christmas so profoundly manifested in such unlikely circumstances as I did on Christmas Day, 1943.

"I was in a British division that was part of the American Fifth Army in Italy. Casualties had been continuous and heavy since we had landed at Salerno. By December, we were advancing slowly north of Naples—cold, very wet, very muddy, quite weary, and a little homesick. Never had the prospect of Christmas seemed so bleak and far away.

"Taking advantage of a lull in the fighting, we decided to take up position on a small farm. The countryside was deserted, so we were surprised as we opened the farmhouse door to find a farmer and his wife and seven children. They invited us to join them for evening soup.

"God had protected them, the farmer told us. The younger children, ranging from two to fourteen, had been huddled in the cellar for days. Two girls had sores on their legs, another had been hit in the back by a piece of shrapnel, and the father's arm was injured. Most of the cattle had been killed, the barn had been burned, and the retreating soldiers had taken their horses, most of their food, and some of their household items. They had no soap, no medical supplies, and very little food, but the house was sound, they were together as a family, and they didn't want to move.

"With their cooperation, we set up a command post in their house. I was a medical orderly, so our commanding officer told me to do what I could for the children. The entire battery was concerned for this family, whose Christmas prospects seemed bleak indeed.

"Without telling them, we collected precious bars of toilet soap, talcum powder, candy, and various odds and ends for the children and their parents. We found a small tree that had been uprooted; it was not a traditional Christmas tree, but we decorated it with silver paper, colored wrappers, and cordite bags. When we had finished, it was the best Christmas tree we had ever seen, decorated with all the love those soldiers wanted to lavish on their own families. At bedtime on Christmas Eve, we could hear the children praying for the English soldiers and their families.

"When we presented our gifts to the parents early Christmas morning, they wept with joy. That Christmas dinner was the first time any of us had had spaghetti for Christmas and the first time the Italians had eaten English Christmas pudding. I will never forget the children's delight over such simple presents, and the hugs and kisses that brought tears to every eye. The family couldn't speak English, and most of us spoke very little Italian, but we all understood that farmer's toast: 'If the spirit that is here now could be in the hearts of all men, this war would never have happened.' For some of those soldiers, it was their last Christmas on earth, and for those of us who survived, it was certainly the most memorable." (Walter Stevenson, "Italy, 1943," *Ensign*, December 1973, p. 14.)

I say a hearty amen to that. Those of us who did survive have never been the same.

Let us all resolve at this special season to let down our dams and retainers and learn to give—freely, willingly.

We may not have a lot of material wealth, but we can give what we have; even more important, we can give ourselves.

May we think seriously about what we need to do in our own lives to let our "rivers" flow freely. As we do so, we'll come to learn the joy of receiving as well.

At this Christmas season, why don't we "get our hearts fixed" so that we can "be give to." The consequences will be wonderful—and eternal.

10

"UNTO THE LEAST..."
☆

Christmas is the season of holly, mistletoe, and counting how many shopping days are left before your bank balance reads zero. Everyone loves the gifts, the surprises, the Christmas secrets whispered behind closed doors, but do you ever find yourself, like me, wishing there was some gift you could give to the Lord? Do you wish you could be like the Wise Men and carry some treasure of special worth into His very presence?

The Lord has given us everything, even our very breath, the life power that sustains every moment of our existence. But what really can we do for Him? He has given us commandments and asked us to obey them. But those commandments are given for our own good. They are given to strengthen us, make us better, and happier. The only thing we can really do for Him, in the final analysis, is to give our love to His children here, to bless and uplift and encourage those souls we meet and live with every day. Every one of them, after all, reaps the stamp of His divine parentage.

In Matthew we read of the love Christ expects us to show others. It says there that on the Day of Judgment the Lord will say this to those who pleased Him:

"For I was an hungered, and ye gave me meat: I was thirsty, and ye gave me drink: I was a stranger, and ye took me in:

"Naked, and ye clothed me: I was sick, and ye visited me: I was in prison, and ye came unto me.

"Then shall the righteous answer him, saying, Lord, when saw we thee an hungered, and fed thee? or thirsty, and gave thee drink?

"When saw we thee a stranger, and took thee in? or naked, and clothed thee?"

And Jesus answered that classic question with this: "Verily I say unto you, Inasmuch as ye have done it unto one of the least of these my brethren, ye have done it unto me." (Matthew 25:35–38, 40.)

We live in a world where high achievement is lauded; we work to develop talents and knowledge; we chase wealth and fame and honor. But all these things mean nothing if we do not develop the highest gift of all—a grand capacity to love our fellows, to hurt when they hurt, to anticipate and meet their unspoken needs.

It is easy, perhaps, to love those we admire. But the truly great soul is he who serves someone who can do nothing for him. As Henry Higgins says to Eliza in *My Fair Lady*, "The greatest secret, Eliza . . . is in having the same manners for all human souls; in short, behaving as though you were in heaven, where there are no third-class carriages, and one soul is as good as another."

Do you give your love in service and sensitivity to the stranger, the less powerful, the poor, the unimportant, the child? Here is a story I heard of a boy named Jim who missed his chance to love someone, someone who desperately needed him.

"The year my father lost his job was a lean one," Jim said. "The electricity was turned off so we used candles. My only sweater had holes and my socks looked like swiss cheese. We had never been poor before, and we didn't know what it was to have to scramble home from school to get the last crust of bread.

"As Christmas approached, only one member in our family had any money," he said. "That was Jerry, who had mowed lawns all summer long to fill the big piggy bank on top of his dresser.

"Let me tell you about Jerry. He was my younger brother, twelve, just a year younger than I, and he was born handicapped. He looked different than my friends and he had the mentality of a six-year-old. He also had a speech problem. His syllables were pronounced incorrectly and his voice was low and gruff.

"When we were very young, we played together, laughed together, learned together, and I didn't see the difference that separated Jerry from the rest of the world. He was my kid brother and I loved him.

"But as the years came along, as I had other friends and played with other children, his difference became noticeable, horrible to me. His difference was an illness, a disease that took him from me, that changed him continuously until he was no longer my brother. Instead he was an embarrassment to me.

"He'd follow me wherever I'd go. When I wanted to play ball with the boys, I couldn't. Nobody wanted Jerry, and that kept me from playing too. I hated him for it. Every moment he seemed to get in the way. One time my hate exploded and I turned on him and said, 'Look, you stupid lookin' creep, why ya gotta follow me around? Leave me alone and go home.' Then I slapped him again and again because I wished he wasn't around. Everyone always called me the one with the M.R. for a brother. He finally went home crying, I didn't care. I was too worried about the chewing out I'd be getting when I got home.

"With Christmas in the air, I only had eyes for one thing. It was a beautiful watch in the jeweler's window, a watch with a gold band. I knew it was impossible but I liked to imagine that Christmas morning would find me wearing it. Every time I passed the shop I'd stare at it forever.

"I woke up Christmas morning rushing to open the one gift that was for me by the fireplace. It was a great-looking sweater, not the watch. 'Thanks a lot, Dad!' I shouted, but I noticed how tired he was. He had been up all night with Jerry, who was sick with pneumonia.

"We walked together into Jerry's room and saw Mom sitting there, her eyes all red with crying. She sniffed softly and said, 'Jerry's got a surprise for you, Jim.' I thought he would give me one of those homemade, butcherpaper, water-colored type of Christmas cards he'd made. He wobbled over to his closet and pulled out his present for me. Just a flat sheet about a square foot big and written in red water color, 'To my big brother: whom I love the most.'

"While I was reading it, I noticed the broken pieces of his piggy bank in the corner. Then he slowly reached under his bed and pulled out a small box. He wiped his nose with his pajama sleeve, then stood there with his arm stretched out, 'Warwy Kwishmas, Shimmy.' I opened the box and there it was, the gleaming reflecting watch with the gold band, the one I thought I'd never see again, couldn't even stop looking at it. Then he gave me a bear hug and asked, 'Shimmy, where my pweshent?' I looked at him, over to the broken pieces of his bank in the corner, at the watch, then back at his questioning eyes, and I didn't even have the courage to tell him I'd forgotten about him. I just grabbed him and cried.

"He never lived to say, 'Happy New Year.' He died two days later."

Though the situation may not be as dramatic, there are those in the world who need you.

The gift at Christmas that the Lord asks of us is to feed His sheep. We are to love His children, even those who are apparently unloveable. We are to look beyond the surface into the soul. To offer the Lord gold and frankincense and myrhh is nothing compared with the gift of a loving heart.

PART 3

Hearing the Message of Christ

11

PRECIOUS GIFTS
☆

As you read the story of the birth of the Savior, have you ever wondered what the gifts of frankincense and myrrh were? I know what gold is, but frankincense and myrrh? As a boy I thought they sounded like super gifts for the Christ child. They sounded unique and mystical and very splendid.

As I matured, my curiosity finally motivated me to do some basic research. I discovered that frankincense is a fragrant substance made from the resin of three different trees. It is sold in the form of "tears," or hardened drops, and is still used today for making incense. In Bible times frankincense was brought by traders from far distant places and, consequently, was very valuable to the people of that day.

I am also better informed about myrrh. Myrrh is found in Eastern Africa and Southern Arabia and is a resin from yet a different kind of tree. It was used as a medicine and cleaning agent, as well as being burned in the temple as a sweet-smelling incense. It was also obtained through traders and had a value equal to that of frankincense.

I am certain that my early Sunday School teacher would be proud of my progress!

As we approach the Christmas season and read once more the story of the Wise Men, it seems appropriate to think again of gold, frankincense, and myrrh. What great gifts! What an acceptable offering for that period! It was undoubtedly the best the Wise Men could provide.

Let us too lay gifts at the feet of the Babe of Bethlehem, hopefully those things that would be the most meaningful to Him. However, since most of us do not possess great wealth, gold, frankincense, and myrrh are perhaps not feasible. I believe our Lord would appreciate gifts from us even more valuable than those precious items. The gifts I have in mind are several He has already requested. He has spoken much about them:

"Then shall the King say unto them on his right hand, Come, ye blessed of my Father, inherit the kingdom prepared for you from the foundation of the world:

"For I was an hungered, and ye gave me meat: I was thirsty, and ye gave me drink: I was a stranger, and ye took me in:

"Naked, and ye clothed me: I was sick, and ye visited me: I was in prison, and ye came unto me.

". . . Verily I say unto you, Inasmuch as ye have done it unto one of the least of these my brethren, ye have done it unto me." (Matthew 25:34–36, 40.)

Well, there they are—gifts for Him that are more valuable than gold; sweeter smelling than frankincense; more healing than myrrh. Let me translate the Lord's request into words we can put into action. Three would say it all: *Care about people.* That is a gift worth giving: "Inasmuch as ye have done it unto one of the least of these my brethren, ye have done it unto me."

The desire to care about people around us is expressed superbly in a verse by Andrew K. Smith:

"If I Could Truly Give"

If I could lift myself from out of me
And freely give to but a single soul
Who craves the warmth of one kind word or deed,
And let his good and pleasure be my goal,
How happy I should be, and so would he,
His craving satisfied, his present need.

If I could truly love another one,
As I now love myself, and really care,
Rejoice with him in his high aims achieved,
His joy would be my own, and I would share
The victory that both of us had won,
The very prize I had for him conceived.

Could I but give my hand in friendliness
To one whom hate and bitterness had chilled,
Add kindly patience for his slow response,
Extend to him until his heart be filled,
Then both of us would then succeed, and bless
The circumstance that filled our mutual wants.

Could I but give myself and consecrate
To Him whose generosity gave me
The wealth of life, the joy of living it,
Here in his world and in eternity,
I then more nearly could appreciate
His gift to me, His love so infinite.

Ezra Taft Benson put into perspective the issue of caring about people when he said, "God has to work through mortals." In other words, if people are going to be helped, we are the ones who must do it. And that's not always easy. Here is an example.

"In spite of the fun and laughter, young Frank Wilson was not happy.

"It was true that he had received all the presents he wanted. And he enjoyed these traditional Christmas Eve reunions of relatives—this year at Aunt Susan's—for the purpose of exchanging gifts and good wishes.

"But Frank was not happy, because this was to be his first Christmas without his brother, Steve, who, during the year, had been the tragic victim of a reckless driver. Frank missed his brother and the close companionship they had enjoyed together.

"He said good-bye to his relatives and explained to his parents that he was leaving a little early to see a friend. Since it was cold outside, Frank put on his new plaid jacket. It was his favorite gift. The other presents he placed on his new sled.

"Then Frank headed for the Flats, hoping to find the patrol leader of his Boy Scout troop. This was the section of town where most of the poor lived, and his patrol leader did odd jobs to help support his family. To Frank's disappointment his friend was not at home, but running errands.

"As Frank hiked down the street, he caught glimpses of trees and decorations in many homes. Although not meaning to pry, suddenly he glimpsed a shabby room with the limp stockings hanging over an empty fireplace. A woman was seated near them weeping. The stockings reminded him of the way he and his brother had always hung theirs side by side. The next morning they would be full of presents. Then he remembered that he had not done his "good turn" for the day.

"He knocked on the door.

" 'Yes?' the sad voice of the woman inquired.

" 'May I come in?'

" 'You are very welcome,' she said, 'but I have no food or gifts for you. I have nothing for my own children.'

" 'That's not why I am here,' Frank replied. 'You are to choose whatever presents you need for your children from this sled.'

" 'Why, God bless you!' the amazed woman answered gratefully.

"She selected some candies, a game, the toy airplane, and a puzzle. When she took the new Scout flashlight, Frank almost cried out. Finally, the stockings were full.

" 'Won't you tell me your name?' she asked, as Frank was leaving.

" 'Just call me the Christmas Scout,' he replied.

"That night Frank saw that his sorrow was not the only sorrow in the world, and before he left the Flats, he had given away the remainder of his toys. The plaid jacket had gone to a shivering boy.

"But he trudged homeward, cold and uneasy. Having given his presents away, Frank now could think of no reasonable explanation to offer his parents. He wondered how he could make them understand.

" 'Where are your presents, son?' asked his father as he entered the house.

" 'I gave them away.'

" 'But we thought you were happy with your gifts.'

" 'I was—very happy,' the boy answered lamely.

" 'But, Frank, how could you be so impulsive?' his mother asked.

"His father was firm. 'You made your choice, Frank. We cannot afford any more presents.'

"His brother gone, his family disappointed in him, Frank suddenly felt dreadfully alone. He had not expected a reward for his generosity for, in the wisdom of young grief, he knew that a good deed always should be its own reward. It would be tarnished otherwise. So he did not want his gifts back. Frank thought of his brother and sobbed himself to sleep.

"The next morning he came downstairs to find his parents listening to Christmas music on the radio. Then the announcer spoke:

" 'Merry Christmas, everybody! The nicest Christmas story we have this morning comes from the Flats. A crippled boy down there has a new sled this morning, another youngster has a fine plaid jacket, and several families report that their children were made happy last night by gifts from a teenage boy who referred to himself as the Christmas Scout. No one could identify him, but the children of the Flats claim that the Christmas Scout was a personal representative of old Santa Claus himself.'

"Frank felt his father's arms go around his shoulders, and he saw his mother smiling through her tears." (*Instructor*, October 1964, p. 414.)

True giving touches all of us, for, as the Savior has taught, if you want to find the real you, lose yourself in the service of others.

May I recommend that we seriously examine ourselves and see what we need to do in order to give that special gift to the Lord. We might start by caring deeply about those around us, especially our own families, and if we do, I guarantee that we will enjoy life more than ever before. Such an offering to Christ will be ever acceptable and is far more meaningful than gold, frankincense, and myrrh. May we all find it so this year.

12

THE SPIRIT OF TAKING
☆

Maybe it's my experience, but I am beginning to like old things: my chair, my comfortable clothes, my golf clubs, my books. Even as a younger man I enjoyed a statement written by Ira Giovanni in A.D. 1513. It was his Christmas message to the world:

"I salute you! There is nothing I can give you which you have not; but there is much, that, while I cannot give, you can take.

"No heaven can come to us unless our hearts find rest in it today. Take heaven.

"No peace lies in the future which is not hidden in the present. Take peace.

"The gloom of the world is but a shadow; behind it, yet within our reach, is joy. Take joy.

"And so, at this Christmas time, I greet you, with the prayer that for you, now and forever, the day breaks and the shadows flee away."

☆

That's a great thought, and one we need in our own day. There *are* some things you and I can take. In fact, we must take them if we're going to find any kind of satisfaction in life.

My generation is sometimes critical of the "now" generation. We sometimes accuse them of being the "gimme" kids. "Gimme this," "Gimme that." And certainly at Christmastime it may seem strange to do so, but there *are* some things we won't receive if we don't take them. Giovanni named three of them: heaven, peace, and joy. Or, in his words:

1. "No heaven can come to us unless our hearts find rest in it today. Take heaven."

2. "No peace lies in the future which is not hidden in the present. Take peace."

3. "The gloom of the world is but a shadow; behind it, yet within our reach, is joy. Take joy."

From my own experience I know that a little bit of heaven is available on earth; peace of mind is possible; joy is all around us. They are there for the taking. We need to pick them up. They are gifts.

Do you remember Wally Purling? If you don't know him you will want to, and perhaps I can introduce you to him. Wally is my kind of young man. He is simple enough to believe that when there is heaven or peace or joy to be had, it's fine to take them. In fact, Wally knows how to create them even when they seem not to exist. Allow me to introduce you to Wally.

"For years now whenever Christmas pageants are talked about in a certain little town in the Midwest, someone is sure to mention the name of Wallace Purling. Wally's performance in one annual production of the nativity play has slipped into the realm of legend. But the old-timers who were in the audience that night never tire of recalling exactly what happened.

"Wally was nine that year and in the second grade, though he should have been in the fourth. Most people in town knew that he had difficulty in keeping up. He was big and clumsy, slow in movement and mind. Still, Wally was well liked by the other children in his class, all of whom were smaller than he, though boys had trouble hiding their irritation when Wally would ask to play ball with them or any game, for that matter, in which winning was important.

"Most often they'd find a way to keep him out but Wally would hang around anyway—not sulking, just hoping. He was always a helpful boy, a willing and smiling one, and the natural protector, paradoxically, of the underdog. Sometimes if the older boys chased the younger ones away, it would always be Wally who'd say, 'Can't they stay? They're no bother.'

"Wally fancied the idea of being a shepherd with a flute in the Christmas pageant that year, but the play's director, Miss Lumbard, assigned him to a more important role. After all, she reasoned, the innkeeper did not have many lines, and Wally's size would make his refusal of lodging to Joseph more forceful.

"And so it happened that the usual large, partisan audience gathered for the town's yearly extravaganza of crooks and crèches, of beards, crowns, halos, and a whole stageful of squeaky voices. No one on stage or off was more caught up in the magic of the night than Wallace Purling. They said later that he stood in the wings and watched the performance with such fascination that from time to time Miss Lumbard had to make sure he didn't wander on stage before his cue.

"Then came the time when Joseph appeared, slowly, tenderly guiding Mary to the door of the inn. Joseph knocked hard on the wooden door set into the painted backdrop. Wally the innkeeper was there, waiting.

" 'What do you want?' Wally said, swinging the door open with a brusque gesture.

" 'We seek lodging.'

" 'Seek it elsewhere.' Wally looked straight ahead but spoke vigorously. 'The inn is filled.'

" 'Sir, we have asked everywhere in vain. We have traveled far and are weary.'

" 'There is no room in this inn for you.' Wally looked properly stern.

" 'Please, good innkeeper, this is my wife, Mary. She is heavy with child and needs a place to rest. Surely you must have some small corner for her. She is so tired.'

"Now, for the first time, the innkeeper relaxed his stiff stance and looked down at Mary. With that, there was a long pause, long enough to make the audience a bit tense with embarrassment.

" 'No! Begone!' the prompter whispered from the wings.

" 'No!' Wally repeated automatically. 'Begone.'

"Joseph sadly placed his arm around Mary and Mary laid her head upon her husband's shoulder, and the two of them started to move away. The innkeeper did not return inside his inn, however. Wally stood there in the doorway watching the forlorn couple. His mouth was open, his brow creased with concern, his eyes filling unmistakably with tears.

"And suddenly this Christmas pageant became different from all others.

" 'Don't go, Joseph,' Wally called out. 'Bring Mary back.' And Wallace Purling's face grew into a bright smile. 'You can have *my* room.'

"Some people in town thought that the pageant had been ruined. Yet there were others—many others—who considered it the most Christmas of all Christmas pageants they had ever seen." (Dina Donohue, "Trouble at the Inn," *Guideposts Magazine*, December 1966.)

That's Wally Purling! When there was a chance for heaven or peace or joy, he simply reached out and took them! No questions asked. He did what he needed to do to bring it about . . . for Mary and Joseph, and for himself.

Now, may I suggest a great secret about taking. If we reach out and take for the right reasons, just as Wally seemed to understand, those around us will be blessed. When we take a bit of heaven, our family enjoys the blessings. When we take peace, we share that gift with everyone else. When we take joy, we take it for others as well as for ourselves. Putting it in a little different way, the great thing about taking is that in doing so, we give.

The Savior is the one who showed us this great secret. The reason he was able to give heaven and peace and joy is that he already possessed them for himself. He took them so that he could give them. How can you and I give something we don't have? Let's take so that we can give!

The spirit of this Christmas secret of taking (and, therefore, giving) is found in a verse by Charles Meigs which I have always enjoyed.

> Lord, help me live from day to day
> In such a self-forgetful way
> That even when I kneel to pray
> My prayer will be for Others.
>
> Help me in all the work I do
> To ever be sincere and true
> And know that all I do for You
> Must needs be done for Others.
>
> Let Self be crucified and slain
> And buried deep, and all in vain
> May efforts be to rise again.
> Unless to live for Others.
>
> And when my work on earth is done
> And my new work in heaven begun
> May I forget the crown I've won
> While thinking still of Others.
>
> Others, Lord, yes Others.
> Let this my motto be:
> Help me live for Others
> That I may live like thee.
> (Charles D. Meigs, "Others," in *Masterpieces of Religious Verse*, ed. James Dalton Morrison [New York: Harper and Row, Publishers, 1948], p. 416.)

I have a friend who was asked in an interview if he was as good a man as his father. His reply was a modest one, simply, "I try to be." To my friend's surprise, the interviewer (who knew both men) replied, "If you're not a better man than your father, he'll be disappointed." And so he would!

We have an obligation to be the best we can be. A loving Heavenly Father expects it of us. And, very frankly, if you and I are going to do that, we've got to take, yes *take*, every advantage we can find to grow and develop. If there's a challenge, let's take it. If there's a task to be done, let's do it. And why? So that by taking and becoming, we can give.

Well, that's one of the secrets of Christmas: the spirit of taking. It is my experience that as we take heaven and peace and joy (and much more), we will be giving, in a very real way, heaven and peace and joy. May it be so with us all.

13

THE LIGHT OF CHRISTMAS
☆

At this season we string up lights against dark streets and celebrate the birth of Jesus Christ. But, you know, even before Christ was born, the inhabitants of the earth observed this season as a special time. Long before precise calendars, long before clocks, all the people who lived in northern Europe could tell that in this season the days grew shorter and shorter, the night ever longer and darker as if the sun itself was dying. Can you be there in imagination with those men and women who depended upon the sun as a source of life and fertility? Can you imagine the fear they must have felt as the earth itself froze, food became scarce, and the sun seemed to dwindle? The Druids sent out runners to the tops of the hill to watch for that moment when the sun had reached its lowest point in the heavens and was ready to return. In Scandinavian countries great fires were kindled to defy the "frost king." These early peoples gathered around fires to comfort one another while they looked forward to the breaking of the ice when their ships might again embark. To these northern people, the sun was considered a wheel which alternately threw its glow upon the earth and away from it. And, oh, what rejoicing at the conclusion of the winter cycle when the sun began to rise over the world with renewed vigor and power after having sunk to its low point in the heavens. We get our word *yule* from this ancient idea of a sun wheel.

I've often thought that though we may have little in common with these ancient, superstitious people, our celebration of Christmas is still a celebration of light's triumph over darkness.

Our Heavenly Father Himself chose to mark the birth of His Son with a new light in the universe. We read in Matthew, "Now when Jesus was born in Bethlehem of Judea in the days of Herod the king, behold, there came wise men from the east to Jerusalem, saying, Where is he that is born King of the Jews? For we have seen his star in the east, and are come to worship him." (Matthew 2:1–2.) Tradition has it that these Wise Men and their fathers and grandfathers before them had watched for the star that meant the Christ was born.

Have you heard the parable of "The Little Star"? Let me relate it to you:

"Once upon a time God created the heaven and the earth. On the first day He said, "Let there be light," and He placed all the stars in the sky—all but one.

"The little star was hurt because it had not been given a chance to shine like the others. But when it went to Him, and wondered why, God replied: 'I'm not ready for you, little star; you must grow some more before I can use you.'

"Many years went by. Then, down on earth one day, the chosen people, the Israelites, escaped from their bondage in Egypt. Their leader was a man named Moses, and he led them between the walls of the river on toward the land of Canaan.

"And our Father in Heaven was very happy about this. He said, 'I need three million stars to form a pillar of fire, to lead my children to the promised land. Who will volunteer? The little star thought, *Now is my chance to shine—I'll volunteer.* But when it came to the Father, He shook His head and told it, 'Not yet, little star: you must become brighter before I can use you.'

"Faster and faster the years passed—all the while the little star was growing larger and brighter. 'When will my time come?' it wondered. On the nights when the clouds hid the other stars from earth, the little star tried to steal beneath the clouds and light the way of the travelers who were lost and could not find their path home. But each time it would be stopped with the words, 'I am not ready to use you, little star: have patience, and some day I will give you your chance.'

"And the little star grieved. 'How much I am missing,' it said as it watched the bigger stars keeping their vigil over David as he slept in the fields at night. 'How I would love to inspire the poets to write their psalms as the other stars do,' the little star sighed as centuries rolled past without a chance for it to shine—but all the while it was growing larger and brighter.

"Then, one day God called to it, 'Little star, the time has come—I am ready to use you.'

"The little star began to shine in anticipation—what was in store for it? As it beamed with satisfaction, the Father placed it in the sky. 'Now, shine, little star'—and shine it did!

"While the star was shining, it noticed that three wise men were looking at it with exceeding joy, as if it held the answer to some question in their minds. Strange to say, the little star felt that it must lead them somewhere. It began to move, and wherever it went, the Wise Men followed.

"As it glided across the sky, the little star noticed that it was headed for a town that lay in the distance. The closer it came to the village, the brighter it beamed. When it reached the edge of the town, the little star burst forth into a radiance which was much more beautiful than any other star ever possessed.

"Suddenly it stopped, directly over a stable. And, as it hovered there, the three Wise Men stepped down from their camels, and they hurried into the stable.

"*What are they looking for?* the little star pondered. From the heavens came the answer, with a voice which said, 'Behold—my Beloved Son.'

"Suddenly, a wonderful peace came over the little star. It knew that its task was done. But it was happy. It had served its purpose, and it was ready to give way to a greater light—a light which was the life of men!"

Do you have need for a light in your life, that steady beacon that charts the way through this dark wilderness that is mortality? Most of us do. We need to know that even when life fragments us and beats us and throws us against personal hazard, we are loved. We yearn for that love and understanding. We need to know that the most powerful being in the universe knows us by name. Paul said, "For I am persuaded, that neither death, nor life, nor angels, nor principalities, nor powers, nor things present, nor things to come, nor height, nor depth, nor any other creature, shall be able to separate us from the love of God, which is Christ Jesus our Lord" (Romans 8:38–39).

Having been mortal, Christ understands, as no one else, the full range of our emotions, our struggles here. His sensitivities took in a broader sweep of both joy and pain than we can imagine—all that He might succor His people. When you kneel at the very limits of your personal extremity, He has been there before you.

Think of His birth. It is a story of poverty. Luke tells us that Mary and Joseph sought refuge for the night, but "there was no room for them in the inn" (Luke 2:7). If they had been richer or more influential or if perhaps they had known the right people, I wonder if a room could have been found for them. Mary, after all, was probably in the first pangs of labor, or at least in great misery, having ridden a long distance on a donkey just as she was ready to deliver.

But no room was found. Not for this birth. How must Mary and Joseph have felt retreating to a stable full of animals to bear God's own child? In thinking of this, a friend of mine, Jeff Holland, said, "I was a student . . . just finishing my first year of graduate work when our first child, a son, was born. We were very poor, though not so poor as Joseph and Mary. My wife and I were both going to school, both holding jobs. . . . We drove a little Volkswagon which had a half-dead battery because we couldn't afford a new one.

"Nevertheless when I realized that our own night of nights was coming, I believe I would have done any honorable thing in this world, and mortgaged any future I had to make sure my wife had the clean sheets, the sterile utensils, the attentive nurses, and the skilled doctors who brought forth our first-born son. If she or that child had needed special care at the Mayo Clinic, I believe I would have ransomed my very life to get it." (Jeffrey R. Holland, "Maybe Christmas Doesn't Come from a Store," *Ensign*, December 1977, pp. 65–65.)

Did Joseph feel any different? What was the sting in his heart as he cleared away the dirty straw and stable litter and prepared a place for Mary to deliver God's own son? Could there be a worse, more disease-ridden spot for a child to be born? Surely for this birth there ought to be scores of attendants to soothe the mother, mop her troubled brow. Surely there should be a doctor to help this Mary, herself hardly more than a child. But none of this was to be. Alone and unattended, without fanfare or mortal notice, Mary brought forth Jesus Christ, the light of the world. There was no sweet linen to wrap the baby in or comfort the exhausted mother, but this was the central point of all human history, and the beginning of a life that was to descend below all things. Why? So that having experienced pain, humiliation, temptation, loneliness, and disappointment, Jesus Christ could be the light at the end of mankind's dark tunnel.

Today there are many who dispute that Jesus Christ was sent from His Father to be a light unto the world, the only light. The so-called philosophical voices among us proclaim Him to be, instead, a great teacher, the son of Mary and Joseph, the greatest moralist of all time, a product of our need to believe, as great as Mohammad, a significant influence on the world. The list goes on. But I bear my witness unto you that Jesus Christ was and is the literal Son of God and the Savior of all mankind. I promise you that if you want to defy darkness, disappointment, doubt, and the forces of uncertainty that seek to drown you, come to know the Lord, Jesus Christ. To all these philosophical voices I say with the angel who stood at His empty tomb, "Why seek ye the living among the dead?" Jesus Christ is not just a historical figure. The Christ who was is the Christ who is. He lives today; He is personal; He has a body. His tomb is empty, a symbol for all of us that no darkness, even death, is so deep we cannot overcome it with His help. We can conquer all. May we so know and understand as we celebrate this Christmas season.

14

CHRISTMAS PARABLES
☆

Our Lord, during his ministry, often taught gospel truths by means of parables. A parable is a short story or saying with a moral or spiritual message. While Jesus did not always employ parables to illustrate His teachings, He became so prolific in their use that Mark records the following: "But without a parable spake he not unto them" (Mark 4:34).

Joseph Klausner, a Jewish author who wrote about Jesus of Nazareth, said that Jesus was a great artist in the use of the parable. He stated that "his parables were attractive, short, popular, drawn from everyday life, full of instruction in wise conduct . . . , simple in form and profound in substance." As Lowell Bennion has noted: "Jesus' parables combine reality with imagination to transform ordinary observations and experience into word-pictures that never existed before."

Those pictures often become identifiable in our daily experiences. Louis Cassels shares one such event in his life.

"Once upon a time, there was a man who looked upon Christmas as a lot of humbug.

"He wasn't a Scrooge. He was a very kind and decent person, generous to his family, upright in all his dealings with other men. But he didn't believe all that stuff about an incarnation which churches proclaim at Christmas. And he was too honest to pretend that he did.

" 'I am truly sorry to distress you,' he told his wife, who was a faithful churchgoer, 'but I simply cannot understand this claim that God became man. It doesn't make any sense to me.'

"On Christmas Eve, his wife and children went to church for the midnight service. He declined to accompany them. 'I'd feel like a hypocrite,' he explained. 'I'd much rather stay at home. But I'll wait up for you.'

"Shortly after his family drove away in the car, snow began to fall. He went to the window and watched the flurries getting heavier and heavier.

" 'If we must have a Christmas,' he reflected, 'it's nice to have a white one.'

"He went back to his chair by the fireside and began to read his newspaper. A few minutes later, he was startled by a thudding sound. It was quickly followed by another, then another. He thought that someone must be throwing snowballs at his living room window.

"When he went to the front door to investigate, he found a flock of birds huddled miserably in the snow. They had been caught in the storm, and in a desperate search for shelter had tried to fly through his window.

"*I can't let those poor creatures lie there and freeze,* he thought. *But how can I help them?*

"Then he remembered the barn where the children's pony was stabled. It would provide a warm shelter. He quickly put on his coat and galoshes and tramped through the deepening snow to the barn. He opened the doors wide and turned on the light. But the birds didn't come in.

"*Food will bring them in,* he thought. So he hurried back to the house for bread crumbs, which he sprinkled on the snow to make a trail into the barn. To his dismay, the birds ignored the bread crumbs and continued to flop around helplessly in the snow. He tried shooing them into the barn by walking around and waving his arms. They scattered in every direction—except into the warm, lighted barn.

" 'They find me a strange and terrifying creature,' he said to himself, 'and I can't seem to think of any way to let them know they can trust me. If only I could be a bird myself for a few minutes, perhaps I could lead them to safety.'

"Just at that moment, the church bells began to ring. He stood silently for a while, listening to the bells pealing the glad tidings of Christmas. Then he sank to his knees in the snow.

" 'Now I understand,' he whispered. 'Now I see why you had to do it.'

Ann Boyles tells this parable:

"There once lived in the city of Marseilles an old shoemaker, loved and honored by his neighbors, who affectionately called him 'Father Martin.' One Christmas Eve, as he sat alone in his little shop reading of the visit of the Wise Men to the infant Jesus, and of the gifts they brought, he said to himself: 'If tomorrow were the first Christmas, and if this Jesus were to be born in Marseilles this night, I know what I would give him!' He rose from his stool and took from a shelf overhead two tiny shoes of softest snow-white leather, with bright silver buckles. 'I would give him these, my finest work.' Then he paused and reflected. 'But I am a foolish old man,' he continued . . . 'The Master has no need of my poor gifts.'

"Replacing the shoes, he blew out the candle and retired to rest. Hardly had he closed his eyes, it seemed, when he heard a voice call his name . . . 'Martin! Martin!' Intuitively he felt a presence. Then the voice spoke again . . . 'Martin, you have wished to see me. Tomorrow I shall pass by your window. If you see me, and bid me enter, I shall be a guest at your table.'

"Father Martin did not sleep that night for joy. And before it was yet dawn he rose and swept and tidied up his little shop. He spread fresh sand upon the floor, and wreathed green boughs of fir along the rafters. On the spotless linen-covered table he placed a loaf of white bread, a jar of honey, and a pitcher of milk.

"When all was in readiness he took up his patient vigil at the window.

"Presently he saw an old street-sweeper pass by, blowing upon his thin, gnarled hands to warm them. 'Poor fellow, he must be half frozen,' thought Martin. Opening the door he called out to him, 'Come in, my friend, and warm yourself, and drink something hot.' And the man gratefully accepted the invitation.

"An hour passed and Martin saw a young, miserably clothed woman, carrying a baby. She paused wearily to rest in the shelter of his doorway. The heart of the old cobbler was touched. Quickly he flung open the door. 'Come in and warm while you rest,' he said to her. 'You do not look well.'

" 'I am going to the hospital. I hope they will take me in, and my baby boy,' she explained. 'My husband is at sea, and I am ill, without [five cents].'

" 'Poor child,' cried Father Martin. 'You must eat something while you are getting warm. No? Then let me give a cup of milk to the little one. Ah! What a bright, pretty little fellow he is! . . . why, you have put no shoes on him!'

" 'I have no shoes for him,' sighed the mother.

" 'Then he shall have this lovely pair I finished yesterday.' And Father Martin took down from the shelf the soft little snow-white shoes he had admired the evening before. He slipped them on the child's feet . . . they fitted perfectly. And shortly the poor young mother went on her way, [some coins] in her hand and tearful with gratitude.

"And Father Martin resumed his post at the window. Hour after hour went by, and although many people passed his window, and many needy souls shared the hospitality of the old cobbler, the expected Guest did not appear.

" 'It was only a dream,' he sighed, with a heavy heart. 'I did hope and believe, but He has not come.'

"Suddenly, so it seemed to his weary eyes, the room was flooded with a strange light. And to the cobbler's astonished vision there appeared before him, one by one, the poor street-sweeper, the sick mother and her child, and all the people whom he had aided during the day. And each smiled at him and said: 'Have you not seen me? Did I not sit at your table?' Then they vanished from his view.

"At last, out of the silence, Father Martin heard again the gentle voice repeating the old familiar words: "Whosoever shall receive one such in my name, receiveth me . . . for I was an hungered, and ye gave me meat; I was thirsty, and ye gave me drink; I was a stranger, and ye took me in. . . . Verily I say unto you, inasmuch as ye have done it unto one of the least of these my brethren, ye have done it unto me.' " (Anne McCollum Boyles, "The Cobbler and His Guest: A Yuletide Legend," from *Sunshine Magazine*, as quoted in *Christmas Readings for the LDS Family*, comp. H. George Bickerstaff [Salt Lake City: Bookcraft, 1967], pp. 43–45.)

That this special season may bring into focus the spiritual truths the Savior taught so well and which our own experiences verify is my prayer.

15

EXPECTATIONS
☆

You may have seen a child open a stack of packages as tall as he is on Christmas morning and then cast weary eyes around and ask, "Is that all?" About that time, parents want to clobber him, but there is something almost universal in that question. We look forward to Christmas Day with such high expectations, thinking a rosy glow will break over our tired hearts, but nothing ever seems to come up to our dreams. Didn't the Christmas tree smell more piney in some far-distant past? Weren't the lights more enchanting? "Is this all?" some part of you may ask. "Is this it?"

When such a thought crosses my mind at this season, I think back to that divine birth almost two thousand years ago. Could there have been a more humble coming? For centuries men had looked to the coming of the Savior. They were expecting a champion who would raise them dramatically from the dust. As George MacDonald wrote,

> They all were looking for a king
> To slay their foes and lift them high.

Thou cam'st a little baby thing
That made a woman cry!
(George MacDonald, "That Holy Thing," *Norman
Rockwell's Christmas Book*, ed. Molly Rockwell
[New York: Harry N.Abrama, Inc.,], p. 24.)

They expected a political king to send oppressive govern-
ments toppling. They expected power in the worldly sense,
the kind of king they already knew, one who would reign
with pomp and wealth. All those who had looked so long to
His birth wanted to be able to grind their enemies down to
size, to conquer, to be at last on the side of the mighty instead
of always being beaten by a world too big for them.

But how did Christ come? He came to a borrowed stable, a
baby whose parents could not even afford adequate medical
help. His clothes were simple, His manner undramatic. He
did not own a home, let alone a palace. He did not take up the
sword to champion His cause. Those who followed Him were
not granted sudden wealth or power over their enemies. In
fact, many of them were commanded to leave all worldly
goods behind them. And when the test came, the ultimate test
in the eyes of the world—how He would stand up against the
mighty Roman government—He was again a disappointment.
He did not come in with a blazing army to tear down the place
and throw His enemies over. No, he meekly submitted to an
unfair judgment and allowed Himself to be crucified. It is not
surprising that there were some who had waited all those
years for the coming of Christ who said, like a child at Christmas, "Is that all? Is this it?" They had been looking for something different.

But how right in every way was the Savior's birth and life!
Could he have understood our human lot if He had been
beyond human concern? What if the mantle of glory had
fallen upon Him all at once? What if His birth had been a
grandiose event accompanied by pomp and circumstance?
"This Is the Child of God," a banner might have said. Would
He then have been as able to walk with us through our sometimes lonely and unrecognized lives? Could He have said with

authenticity, "I know," when we cry against our pain? You see, wherever we've been, on whatever dark road we've walked and shivered in our fright, He's been there too. He knows what it is to be forsaken by friends, to have His best efforts mocked. He knows what it is to be hungry, to be tempted, to be so weary He could hardly take another step. When you kneel at the very limits of your endurance, He has been there before you.

Endurance. Jenny Walker knew all about that as she walked along the main street that led to Peterson's store. It had been an early winter in the Depression, and now Christmas was near. And though she was only thirty-two, she felt like an old woman, her cares like an extra weight that made her body heavy as she walked along. Her husband had been gone a month now, out trying to find work with the construction crews working along the road. He had been a sheep man, but the hard times and the early winter had not been kind to them. They had watched their sheep drop dead one by one in the harsh climate until their flock had been decimated. With those sheep went their dreams—so much for youth's bright hopes.

"I think I can earn enough to meet the mortgage payments so we can at least keep the farm," Jenny's husband had said. Then he'd gone, leaving her and five children to make their way. She hadn't heard from him since. Was it just the mail? She knew how irregular the mail was at Christmas.

The bell over the door jingled with a merry sound as Jenny walked into Peterson's Store. It was Christmas itself inside with the heavy smell of gingerbread and pine in the air. Children were clustered around the table in the center of the country store. This table—which might sit unnoticed in a corner, covered with farm tools or flour sacks during the rest of the year—was now the center of interest for the little town during the weeks just before Christmas; for then, just once a year, the store carried toys. The day the toys arrived the children could hardly sit still in school. Some lucky one would get the word first that the toys had arrived and the word would spread like magic. Dolls with painted faces and painted hair, and maybe for some little girl, a doll with real hair that curled around her face. Tinkertoys and blocks and pocket knives for the boys. Jenny listened to the children "ooh" and "ah" and watched them shine with excitement as they stood before the loaded table. And she caught a familiar face among them, too. Her own nine-year-old Tad was there wondering what he'd get for Christmas, just as excited and hopeful as the rest of them.

She had to turn her head quickly and blink back the tears to keep from crying. There was simply no money for Christmas this year—not enough for a twenty-five-cent doll to stick in a matchbox, not enough to buy the sugar to make honey candy. There was not enough money for the mortgage payment and her husband was . . . she didn't know where. She traded the eggs she'd brought for some flour to make bread and headed home. She was sure that no one on the face of the earth was more miserable than she. "Oh, God, what have I ever done wrong that You would reject me so?" she prayed on the way home. She wondered if her faith had always been misplaced. Certainly all her best efforts in life had come to nothing.

Christmas Eve brought a blizzard to the town where Jenny lived. Inside their home, she did her best to build a fire, sing Christmas carols, and make the children feel a sense of the season. But she could hardly bear it when Tad came running in with his sock to hang by the fireplace and the little ones followed along. "I don't think Santa can find us in this weather," she'd tried to say, looking at the five empty socks along the fireplace. "Santa can do anything," Tad had assured her, and then he trotted off to bed and went to sleep with that same Christmas shine.

Jenny sat before the socks late into the night wondering what to do and where her family could go when they lost their farm. She tried to pray again but decided that maybe God was just too busy to bother with her, and she fell asleep on the couch in front of the five sagging socks.

Suddenly a noise awoke her. How long she'd been asleep she did not know. Someone was inside her house. She picked up a log to arm herself against the intruder, when she heard the sweetest sound she'd ever known. "Jenny?" said the voice. It was her husband. "Oh, Jenny, I'm sorry. I would have done anything to get here sooner," he said. "But to get here at all I had to catch a ride with a trucker and then walk the last eight miles from the turnoff to town."

"I haven't heard from you for so long," Jenny said as she rushed to where her husband stood.

"We don't have mail service along the road," he said. "Did you think you were alone, that I'd ever leave you alone?"

Jenny thought about that as he put a small toy in each of the five socks. And for Tad, a new pocket knife. But for Jenny the Christmas gift was not small. It was the message that repeated itself over and over in her head, "Did you think I'd ever leave you alone?" It seemed to be a message, not just from her husband, but from the Lord Himself: "You are never alone."

Let that be your Christmas message this year. You are never alone. When any of us is tempted to look for Christ to enter our lives in some dazzling way, when we expect Him to come and crush our dragons, we may be looking for the wrong thing. And like the child at Christmas, we may end up saying, "Is that all?" No, that is not all. Christ came as a baby and as a man walked the path with all its wounds so that He might silently hold our hand when we walk our own rugged path. He is there even when our voice seems to echo back to us in the silence. Could a rich and glittering king have ever done that? That the true meaning of Christmas be ours is my sincere prayer.

INDEX
☆